D1474902

Published by

THE BIBLE FOR TODAY PRESS
900 Park Avenue
Collingswood, New Jersey 08108
U.S.A.

December, 1997

Copyright, 1997
All Rights Reserved

ISBN #1-56848-010-5

ACKNOWLEDGMENTS

        This is to acknowledge the help of Mrs. R. E. Cosby who transcribed the author's comments on the various issues that were raised in the course of these Video/Telecasts. The comments were first made on the weekly thirty-minute radio program, THE BIBLE FOR TODAY OF THE AIR. All 36 of these broadcasts are available as **BFT/110-118 @ $30.00 +P&H**. There are 9, 2-hour cassettes totaling 18 hours in all. I have edited these comments as needed for this present manuscript form. Thanks also to Yvonne S. Waite (Mrs. D.A.) and to our Assistant to the Bible For Today Director, Mr. Daniel S. Waite for their helpful suggestions. A special word of thanks goes to Dr. Kirk D. DiVietro for his faithful assistance on various computer questions. DAW

A Supplemental Sequel to
Defending the King James Bible

FOREWORD

• This book, *Foes of the King James Bible Refuted*, is important because of the various arguments that have been set forth against both the King James Bible and the Hebrew and Greek texts that underlie it. Such arguments have arisen in the past, are arising in the present, and will arise in the future.

• Here are refutations of some of the leading foes of the Grand Old Version, the King James Bible. These include a television personality, a spokesman for the New International Version, a spokesman for the New American Standard Version, a spokesman for the New King James Version, a professor from Dallas Theological Seminary, and an anti-King James Bible author.

• Their arguments are not new. They have been around ever since the days of Bishop Brooke Foss Westcott and Professor Fenton John Anthony Hort and their forerunners. Look at the **principles** discussed in this book, rather than at the **personalities** involved.. There are many additional things that could be said on any given subject touched upon in this book. These answers are offered in somewhat abbreviated form so that there can be an interaction with the subject matter without further delay.

• The book is completely indexed for the convenience of the readers so that they can turn immediately to any subject or person that might interest them. There is also a Scripture index to enable the readers to find information on the various verses that were mentioned.

Sincerely yours for God's Words,

D. a. Waite

Rev. D. A. Waite, Th.D., Ph.D.
Director, The Bible For Today, Incorporated

TABLE OF CONTENTS

SECTION   PAGE

Foes

of the
King James Bible

Refuted

John Ankerberg--Host
Kenneth Barker--NIV Committee
Don Wilkins--NASV Committee
Arthur Farstad--NKJV Committee
Dan Wallace--DTS Professor
James White--Author

By Rev. D. A. Waite, Th.D., Ph.D.

Director, THE BIBLE FOR TODAY, INCORPORATED
900 Park Avenue, Collingswood, NJ 08108
Phone: 609-854-4452; FAX: 609-854-2464;
Orders: 1-800-JOHN 10:9; E-Mail: BFT@BibleForToday.org

B.F.T. #2777

From the Official Script of
The John Ankerberg Video/Telecasts
Summer and Fall, 1995
Re-Broadcast Summer of 1997

INTRODUCTORY COMMENTS

A.   What This Is. This is an analysis of the John Ankerberg Television show entitled "Which English Translation of the Bible Should Christians Use?" It was aired in part during the Summer and Fall of 1996. Some of the telecasts were re-run the summer of 1997 as well, according to a report received. Though not all of the material was used on the 1996 television programs (according to those who listened), the entire debate was preserved on video tape and was offered to John Ankerberg's audience together with the Script of these programs.

B.   Why Was this Made? The following analysis and refutation is taken from the official John Ankerberg Script. Since some of the prominent leaders of the new Bible versions were guests of the program, I feel it is important to answer some of their errors in both fact and opinion so that those of us who use and favor the King James Bible might be prepared to answer such objections when we read them or hear them offered in some way from others.

C.   How Did It Come to Pass? The entire refutation is available on nine, two-hour cassettes. This is **B.F.T. 110-118** for a GIFT to the Bible for Today of **$27.00**. Mrs. R. E. Cosby, took the eighteen hours of material found on these nine cassettes and typed out my responses to key questions raised by the opponents of the King James Bible. She put this all on computer disk so that I could edit it and make this booklet for others to read. I appreciate the many hours of work that she did in this project.

D.   How Is the Ankerberg Script Arranged?   The Script of the video/telecasts was printed by Dr. John Ankerberg on 55 pages of 8 ½" by 11" paper. Five pages of "Glossary" have been added at the end of the Script, making a total of 60 pages in all. The eight recorded programs are found as follows in the Script:

1.   **Program #1**, pages 1-6.
2.   **Program #2**, pages 6-12.
3.   **Program #3**, pages 12-17.
4.   **Program #4**, pages 17-24.
5.   **Program #5**, pages 24-31.
6.   **Program #6**, pages 31-36.

7. **Programs #7 and #8**, pages 36-55.

8. **Glossary**, pages 1-5 at the end of the Script.

E. What Method Is Used in this Study? My method in analyzing the major points of these video/telecasts will be to take up the programs one at a time, and make comments on the salient points of each. I will give a brief summary of the point made by John Ankerberg's guests and then give my comments. All page numbers refer to the official John Ankerberg Script .

F. The Participants on the Programs and How Long Each Talked. To figure out how long each participant talked, I took an approximate measure in inches of space each took in the Script. Since John Ankerberg told me they only talk 20 minutes on each of his 30 minute programs and there were eight programs, I figured 8 x 20' is equal to 160 minutes in all for the entire Script. I then converted the inches of space into percentages of time and arrived at the approximate minutes each speaker spoke. The ones with the "-" after their names were **AGAINST** the King James Bible and the Textus Receptus that underlies it. The ones with the "+" after their names were **FOR** the King James Bible and the Textus Receptus that underlies it.

	NAMES	INCHES	PERCENT	MINUTES
1.	John Ankerberg -	168"	26%	42'
2.	James White -	112"	17%	27'
3.	Dan Wallace -	88"	14%	22'
4.	Kenneth Barker -	76"	12%	19'
5.	Samuel Gipp +	67"	10%	16'
6.	Joseph Chambers +	54"	8%	13'
7.	Arthur Farstad -	42"	6%	10'
8.	Don Wilkins -	28"	4%	6'
9.	Thomas Strouse +	21"	3%	5'
	9 speakers	**656"**	**100%**	**160 minutes**

G. An Assessment of "Fairness" to the King James Bible's Side of the Debate. If you add up the totals for the six participants against the King James Bible, you get this:

	INCHES	PERCENT	MINUTES
Anti-KJB	514"	79%	126'
Pro-KJB	142"	21%	34'
	656"	100%	160'

This is in spite of the fact that John Ankerberg promised me that there would be an attempt at **"FAIRNESS"** of time given to each side if I were to have been on the program as originally invited. The results of this tabulation are obvious.

I.
COMMENTS ON PROGRAM #1
Script, Pages 1-6

Accuracy

#1 Issue: John Ankerberg, the host, asked which one of the versions, New International Version (NIV), New American Standard Version (NASV), New King James Version (NKJV), or the King James Bible (KJB) was "the most accurate." As the host of the program, it is understandable that he took the greatest number of inches of the Script. He ranked 1st out of 9 in total number of inches in the entire Script, that is 168" out of a possible 656." This is 26% of the time which translates into 42 minutes out of the 160 minute total. (Script, p. 1)

Comment by Dr. Waite: The King James Bible is the most accurate English Bible. It has superior texts of Hebrew and Greek, superior translators, superior translation technique, and superior theology.

#2 Issue: John Ankerberg took no sides on which was the "most accurate." (Script, p. 1)

Comment by Dr. Waite: Which version does John Ankerberg use? What version would he say is the most accurate? Though he didn't say it here, in another article appearing in his newsletter, he opposed the King James Bible in many areas. I'm sure he would say that either the New International Version, the New American Standard Version, the New King James, or some version other than the King James Bible was the most accurate. We have answered his opposition to the King James Bible as it appeared in his newsletter. He attacked both the King James Bible and especially the New Testament Greek text that underlies it. This answer is available as **B.F.T./ #95-98** for a GIFT to the Bible for Today of **$12.00 + P&H**. These are 16 radio broadcasts and are contained on four, two-hour tapes.

Dr. Samuel Gipp

#3 Issue: John Ankerberg said "I'd like to start with you, Dr. Samuel Gipp." (Script, p. 1)

Comment by Dr. Waite: First John Ankerberg turned to Dr. Samuel C. Gipp. Dr. Gipp is one of the three that stands for the King James Bible. Dr. Gipp takes a different position than I take in some of these areas as we'll see. He follows Dr. Peter Ruckman's position on the King James Bible. He was asked by John Ankerberg to be on the program because Dr. Ruckman, for one reason or another, turned down his request. He was on the program as a representative of Dr. Ruckman's position. This is one of the reasons why I did not choose to appear on the program. Dr. John Ankerberg asked me to be one of the participants, and after careful questioning of him at length, I at first agreed to be on the program. He had told me that Dr. Gipp would not appear. It would then be an honest and objective discussion of the relative accuracy and worth of the KJB, NKJV, NASV and NIV with the leading proponents of each presenting their positions. I was in favor of that. Within a week, however, of the time Dr. Ankerberg had agreed to this format, he sent me a letter announcing that Dr. Gipp would be on the program. I then wrote John Ankerberg canceling my appearance. He called me and told me that his board of directors insisted that a representative of the Ruckman position be on the program.

From this I could see that it was going to be a "hatchet job" against the King James Bible and it would be putting all of the King James Bible men in the same position as Dr. Ruckman's position which is extreme in many areas in the King James battle. I could see also that much of the time on the programs would be spent in refuting these extreme positions rather than being able to attack the textual errors, the translational errors, and the theological errors of the NIV, NASV and the NKJV. As noted above, Dr. Gipp ranked 5th out of 9 in total number of inches in the entire Script, that is 67" out of a possible 656." This is 10% of the time which translates into only 16 minutes out of the 160 minute total. He spoke out frequently, and in some cases at least, I would agree with what he was saying. There were many other cases, as we will see in this report, where he was seriously in error.

Greek or English Source?

#4 Issue: John Ankerberg asked Dr. Gipp why he thought the KJB was a "perfect" translation and why when people translate the Bible into other languages, he suggests they use the King James Bible (KJB) rather than any Greek text. (Script, p. 1)

Comment by Dr. Waite: I do not agree with this premise if this is Dr. Gipp's premise. I believe that the premise should be: if you know the Greek and Hebrew language you should compare those languages with the language into which you are translating. Now it's obvious, if you don't know Greek and Hebrew and you are trying to translate into some foreign language, the King James Bible in English is certainly the most accurate one to go by. I would agree with that, but try always to compare it with the Hebrew and Greek that underlies our King James Bible.

KJB or TR?

#5 Issue: Dr. Gipp said: "You are going to find places where the *King James Bible* doesn't agree with even the *Textus Receptus* or something like that, so I believe the King James Bible is the *preserved* Word of God." (Script, p. 1)

Comment by Dr. Waite: He is favoring the King James Bible as over against the *Textus Receptus* Geek text that underlies it. This is wrong. This is the false, erroneous Ruckman position to take the English King James Bible and correct the Hebrew and Greek text on which it is based. In my considered opinion, this can be none other than heresy. You can **never** correct the original text of Hebrew and Greek that God authored and has preserved with English, Spanish, French or any other translation. This is one of the very heresies with which John Ankerberg and others on his program wanted to tarnish all who hold to the King James Bible. He wanted to make it look like all of us who hold to that Bible believe as Dr. Gipp that the King James Bible can disagree even with the *Textus Receptus* which is the Greek text from which it was taken. Dr. Gipp could also have said that he believes that the King James Bible corrects even the Masoretic Hebrew Text from which it was translated. I believe that the King James Bible is an excellent translation. It is the most accurate translation from the Greek and Hebrew texts that underlie it. But you cannot corrupt and change the Greek and Hebrew text and correct it with the English King James Bible or any other language version. This is illogical, unscriptural, and should never be done.

I believe that those Hebrew manuscripts that underlie the King James Bible have been preserved by God Himself in keeping with His promise in Psalm 12:6-7 and many other verses. This is called the Masoretic Traditional Hebrew Text edited by Ben Chayyim in the 1520's. Since, as I believe, God preserved His original Hebrew Words by means of these accurate copies, these copies give us the very words that God gave to the original writers of the Old Testament such as Moses, David, Samuel, and the others.

In the same manner, I believe that the Greek manuscripts that underlie the King James Bible have been preserved by God Himself in keeping with His promise in Psalm 12:6-7 and many other verses. This is called the Traditional Greek Text or the *Textus Receptus* from Beza's 5th edition in 1598. Since, as I believe, God preserved His original Greek Words by means of these accurate copies, these copies give us the very words that God gave to the original writers of the New Testament such as Matthew, Mark, Luke, John, Paul, Peter, James, and the others.

I believe that those Hebrew and Greek words God has preserved for us. He promised to preserve His words. I believe He has preserved them in those Hebrew and Greek manuscripts that we have today. The King James Bible in 1611 was translated accurately, professionally, reliably, and in a sound theological manner from those original language manuscripts. We cannot change those original language manuscripts by the King James Bible and try to correct them that way and say they give us some "advanced revelation." This is the position that Dr. Peter Ruckman and Dr. Samuel Gipp have taken and I believe that this is wrong.

Must a Russian Learn the English Bible?

#6 Issue: John Ankerberg asked Dr. Gipp: "If a guy is in Russia and he really wants to get to the truth of the Word of God, would he have to learn English?" Dr. Gipp answered: "Yes." (Script, pp. 1-2)

Comment by Dr. Waite: This position once again represents serious error. This is the position of Dr. Ruckman and Dr. Gipp and their followers. They believe that the King James Bible in English is the only language that God has reserved, and the only thing that should be used today. Their argument goes something like this: God wrote the Old Testament in one language, Hebrew. He wrote the New Testament in one language, Greek. Today, since English is the predominant language of the world, it is the English King James Bible that should be used. For this reason, Dr. Gipp said that the man in Russia would have to learn English "to get the truth of the Word of God." The implication is that he would have to use the King James Bible rather than an accurate translation into the Russian language. This is a strange answer. Romans 16:26, speaking of the *"gospel"* which was a hidden mystery in the Old Testament, says:

> *"But now is made manifest, and by the scriptures of the prophets, according to the commandment of the everlasting God, __made known to all nations__ for the obedience of faith:"*

This verse implies that the Scriptures which are *"made known to all nations"* should be in their own heart language or mother tongue so they can have *"the obedience of faith."* I believe that God is interested in having His Words translated accurately into the languages of every person in this world. The translation must be taken from the proper Hebrew and Greek texts. The translators must be proficient, professional, and able. The technique of translation must have verbal equivalence and have the forms of the words equivalent wherever possible. The theology must be sound and accurate as well.

God does not restrict His Words and His Truth to the English language. Do you understand the error of Samuel Gipp when he says in order to know "the truth of the Word of God" you have to know English? That is serious heresy and error. We want God's Hebrew and Greek Words translated accurately into every language in the world. Sad to say, this is not presently being done by the United

Bible Societies, the American Bible Society, the Wycliffe Translators, or similar groups These groups use erroneous Bible texts of Hebrew and Greek, erroneous techniques of translation, resulting in erroneous and heretical theology.

Do you remember the Day of Pentecost in Acts Chapter 2. God the Holy Spirit performed a miracle on the 12 apostles that were there. Here the Jews were gathered from every corner of the globe for the feast of Pentecost. They needed the gospel of Christ. There were at least 12 different languages present from all over the then-known world. These Jews had to receive the gospel of our Savior in their own language. Now, God did not make those people learn the Hebrew, the language of the Old Testament. He did not make them learn Greek, the language of the New Testament. He performed a miracle of languages or tongues. He permitted each one of those 12 apostles to preach and teach in the 12 different languages of the people who were gathered there on that feast day. They preached the gospel in those languages so that the people understood their own languages. God performed that miracle so that the gospel could go out. The people wondered how they heard the gospel in their own language. I think that this illustrates that God wants His Truth in all the languages of the world including those that were gathered on the Day of Pentecost.

When Samuel Gipp says that English is the only way to go and that the English corrects, gives "advanced revelation," and at times even contradicts the Hebrew and Greek, we believe that this is total heresy. God's Word in Hebrew and Greek are the very words that God spoke to the original writers, gave to us through accurate copies, and preserved for us down to the present age. To say that the only word that God has preserved for us is in English and not preserved in Hebrew and Greek and that everyone who wants to know the Word of God must learn English is blatant heresy and perversion of truth.

"Inspired" and "Preserved"

#7 Issue: Dr. Don Wilkins from the New American Standard Version (NASV) committee, said that Dr. Gipp takes it on faith that the King James Bible is "inspired." Actually Dr. Gipp stated: "I don't call it the 'inspired' Word of God, I call it the 'preserved' Word of God." As noted above, Don Wilkins ranked 8th out of 9 in total number of inches in the entire Script, that is 28" out of a possible 656." This is 4% of the time which translates into only 6 minutes out of the 160 minute total. (Script, p. 1)

Comment by Dr. Waite: What does "inspired" or "inspiration" mean? The word, "inspiration," occurs only one time in the Greek New Testament. It is found only in 2 Timothy 3:16. The Greek word means "God-breathed." What did God breathe out? God "breathed out" His inerrant, infallible Words of the Old Testament in Hebrew (and a few verses in Aramaic.) God "breathed out" His inerrant, infallible Words of the New Testament in Greek. That is what He "inspired." This is the primary meaning of the word "inspiration." He did not "breathe out" languages such as: Spanish, French, German, Chinese, Japanese, Russian, or even English. These versions of the Bible all come to us as "translations" from the preserved copies of what were originally God-breathed, inspired, infallible, inerrant Hebrew and Greek Words

---

#8 Issue: Don Wilkins and Samuel Gipp were arguing about "inspiration" and "preservation." Samuel Gipp said: "He (that is, God) said it was preserved." I suppose he was referring to the KJB. (Script, p. 2)

Comment by Dr. Waite: God never said His Words were to be Preserved in English or in other languages other than those in which they were originally written--Hebrew/Aramaic and Greek.. Samuel Gipp referred to Psalm 12:6-7 He wrongly interpreted these words to refer to the King James Bible in the English language. The promised Preservation, on the other hand, refers to the Hebrew Words of the Old Testament and, by analogy, to the Greek Words of the New Testament:

> Psalm 12:6-7 *"**The words of the LORD** [are] pure words: [as] silver tried in a furnace of earth, purified seven times. **Thou shalt keep them**, O LORD, **thou shalt preserve them** from this generation for ever."*

It is not the English words, French words, Spanish words, Italian words, or other language words that He promised to preserve. These languages were not even in existence when Psalm 12:6-7 was written. Now, it's true that the King James Bible translated the Preserved words of the Hebrew and Greek by rendering them accurately into English, thus "preserving" them in that sense. But the Preservation of the words mentioned in Psalm 12:6-7, strictly speaking, refers to the Old Testament Hebrew Words, and, by extension, to the New Testament Greek Words-- not to English words.

#9 Issue: Dr. Gipp repeated that God was "preserving" His Words in English rather than Latin or other languages. (Script, p. 2)

Comment by Dr. Waite: Notice what John Ankerberg is doing on this program. He had promised me on his word that if I were to come on the program, I would represent the King James Bible position. He would have representatives for the New International Version, for the New American Standard Version, and for the New King James Version. We would all defend our own version. We would discuss the issues on a high level. There wouldn't be any lightening rods, or an attack on the Ruckman position, because it would not be present. There would be solid argumentation on the basis of evidence. On that basis, I agreed to be a participant on the programs.

As I mentioned before, John Ankerberg promised me that Dr. Gipp would not be on the program. I agreed to come on, but then the next day a letter came to me saying that Dr. Ankerberg had invited Dr. Samuel Gipp to be on the broadcast. John Ankerberg went back on his word to me. I wrote him a letter saying that I could no longer be on the broadcast because he had lied to me and gone back on his word. He had not done what he originally told me he would do. I told him that I knew what he was going to do. He was going to help to smear with Dr. Gipp's and Dr. Ruckman's false positions everyone who stands for the King James Bible. This is not, in my opinion, honest, however much it might help attract an audience. My prediction to John Ankerberg as to what would happen has come to pass. John Ankerberg had Samuel Gipp to lead off the discussion in a successful attempt to bring out some silly argument which the other anti-King James Bible men could then move in like sharks after Samuel Gipp and after the King James Bible. This is why I did not want to be a part of this program. I did not want to partake in a "knock-down-drag-out-fight" which is how it turned out.

Preserving the Bible--What Language?

> **#10 Issue:** Dr. Gipp talked of Hebrew as being the language of the Old Testament, Greek being the language of the New Testament, and English being the language of the modern world, hence "Preserving" the Bible in English was the most important today. (Script, p. 2)

Comment by Dr. Waite: Here Dr. Gipp talked about only preserving the Bible in English, not in any other language. This is a false position. It is against the Word of God. I have commented in detail about this in **#7, #8, and #9 Issues** above. (Script, p. 2)

> **#11 Issue:** John Ankerberg then turned to Dr. Thomas Strouse to whom he said, "you would take a little different position than Samuel. Would you tell us what that is?" (Script, p. 2)

Comment by Dr. Waite: Dr. Thomas Strouse is a member of the Advisory Council of our Dean Burgon Society. He is a man who knows the Greek Text and stands with us in this area.

> **#12 Issue:** Dr. Strouse spoke briefly about the Authorized Version reflecting "the providential preservation of God through the original languages of the *Masoretic Text* and *Textus Receptus* is a position of faith." (Script, p. 2)

Comment by Dr. Waite: If you had a Script, you would notice that Dr. Thomas Strouse did not get anywhere nearly as long to speak as Samuel Gipp or as long as James White. Though James White had nothing to do with any of the three versions whose leaders are on the program, nevertheless he was permitted to speak 2nd only in length to John Ankerberg, the host. James White ranked 2nd out of 9 in total number of inches in the entire Script, that is 112" out of a possible 656." This is 17% of the time which translates into 27 minutes out of the 160 minute total. On the other hand, as noted above, Dr Strouse ranked 9th out of 9 in total number of inches in the entire Script, that is 21" out of a possible 656." This is 3% of the time which translates into only 5 minutes out of the 160 minute total. Dr. Thomas Strouse had about 4 inches of type on this occasion. John Ankerberg cut him off. Dr. Strouse had much more to say and he is saying it straight, but John Ankerberg interrupted him. It is evident that John Ankerberg's purpose was not to let the sound position defending the King James Bible and its underlying Hebrew and Greek texts be explained carefully to his audience. He only wanted to smear and berate the position of Dr. Gipp and Dr. Ruckman.

Which Manuscripts?--a "Ton of Others"

#13 Issue: John Ankerberg asked Dr. Strouse "How did you know that those [the Masoretic Hebrew and Textus Receptus Greek] are the superior ones that God preserved because there's a ton of others?" (Script, p. 3)

Comment by Dr. Waite: I would have answered this as follows: "Tons of manuscripts other than those that stand for the King James Bible?" I would have confronted John Ankerberg right up front. I would have said:

> *"Do you realize, Mr. Ankerberg, that of the 5,255 manuscripts (81 Papyrus Fragments, 267 Uncial Manuscripts, 2,764 Cursive Manuscripts, 2,143 Lectionary Manuscripts) of the Greek language that we have, as of 1967, (according to Kurt Aland in Munster, Germany, an archenemy of the Textus Receptus), less then 1% go along with the text that you support? This is B and ℵ, (Vatican and Sinai) and about 43 other manuscripts. There are about 5,210 manuscripts that go along with the King James Bible (over 99% of the evidence)."*

How can John Ankerberg say that there are "a ton of others"? 1% is not a ton! For further documentation on these numbers, see page 56 (5th printing) of my book *DEFENDING THE KING JAMES BIBLE* available as **B.F.T. #1594-P @ $12+$4 P&H**. Those who follow the Westcott and Hort false Greek text (now called the Nestle-Aland text or the United Bible Societies text) use basically manuscript B (Vatican) and ℵ (Sinai) and only about 43 others. Where is their "ton"? What good would that "ton" do since they don't bother with over 99% of the evidence?

NIV--Best Selling Bible?

#14 issue: John Ankerberg, talking with Dr. Kenneth Barker of the New International Version Committee said: "And so by actual cash register counts right now, it [the NIV] is by far the best-selling Bible going." (Script, p. 3)

Comment by Dr. Waite: Do you consider the New International Version a **Bible**? I do not consider the New International Version a Bible. I consider it a version. It is filled and loaded with paraphrase and perversion, regardless of "cash register counts." I found in my study of the New International Version 6,653 examples of dynamic equivalency. Because I had already taken two years and eight months and my computer was filling up, I stopped counting at 6,653 examples. There are thousands and thousands more. These were examples of adding to God's Words, subtracting from God's Words, or changing God's Words in some other manner. This is a **perversion** of a Bible, not a Bible! This is 284 pages of research. It is available as **B.F.T. #1749-P** for a GIFT to B.F.T. of **$25 + $4 P&H.**

#15 Issue: John Ankerberg said to Dr. Barker, "And, well, another 50 years and the fact is you will have superseded all the Bibles that have been sold in the last whatever number of years, 400 years from the time of the 1611." (Script, p. 3)

Comment by Dr. Waite: As noted above, Kenneth Barker ranked 4th out of 9 in total number of inches in the entire Script, that is 76" out of a possible 656." This is 12% of the time which translates into 19 minutes out of the 160 minute total.

In "another 50 years," this will not be the same version. The New International Version in another 50 years will have had 5 different, distinct editions. According to Kenneth Barker's own testimony, every 10 years the New International Version is going to change. It will not be the same thing. This will not be comparing apples with apples or bananas with bananas. It will be comparing grapes with figs or onions with potatoes. You cannot say that the same version will have sold many million of copies, because it will be a completely different version. Anyone can see if you take a Ford car that is a 1945 model and you sell so many millions of those Ford cars and then in 1955, 1965, 1995 you sell so many more millions of those models and you say, "Oh, we have sold so many millions of Fords!" That's true, but it's not the same model Ford at all. It is a different model every year. This is how it is with the New International Version, it is a different model every 10 years. So, you cannot say that those statistics are going to be the same as applied to the King James Bible that has not changed and will not change from now until the next 50 years, or until the Lord Jesus Christ will come.

#16 Issue: Dr. Barker said: "John, I'm glad that you mentioned that it [that is, the NIV] is the best-selling Bible . . ." (Script, p. 3)

Comment by Dr. Waite: Kenneth Barker has the greatest number of inches of Script space, more than any other guest thus far. I'd say that John Ankerberg is leaning in favor of Dr. Barker. James White has about 6 inches of space. Dr. Strouse has about 4 inches. Dr. Gipp had about 6 inches of space, but here Dr. Barker has 11 full inches to talk about his point of view. Kenneth Barker's total, as mentioned above, was 75" of Script space which is 12% of the time, or 19 minutes in all. Is this fair? Of course it was not!

#17 Issue: Kenneth Barker said that the NIV had "approximately 100 million NIV Bibles and New Testaments in world-wide circulation and use." (Script, p. 3)

Comment by Dr. Waite: Kenneth Barker said the NIV had sold 100 million "Bibles and New Testaments." The King James Bible is the entire Bible Genesis through Revelation. Here, Kenneth Barker is able to throw in the New Testaments separately as well as the entire Bibles. This does not compare apples to apples again.

#18 Issue: Kenneth Barker repeated that the NIV was the "best-selling Bible." (Script, p. 3)

Comment by Dr. Waite: I dispute those statistics. I know there are many who have said that the New International Version is presently out-selling the King James Bible. This has been disputed in David Cloud's paper, *O' Timothy*. He said that the statistics that are used are simply from one distribution house (Spring Arbor) and do not consider other Bible distributors that are using and selling the King James Bible as well. Certainly it does not include the "Bearing Precious Seed" groups all over this country that have their own giant web presses that print King James Bibles by the 100,000's each year (even millions)! These Bibles are not sold in bookstores, but by the churches (most of them are Baptist Churches) throughout this country. So, I would dispute that the New International Version is the best selling translation of the Bible today.

The NIV's Hebrew & Greek Texts

#19 Issue: Kenneth Barker said: "We based it [the NIV] on the *Masoretic* or traditional Hebrew text in the Old Testament and on what could be called an eclectic text that you find in New Testaments . . ." (Script, p. 3)

Comment by Dr. Waite: That's not true! They most certainly did **not** base the NIV **exclusively** on the Masoretic Hebrew text in the Old Testament. Yet this is what Dr. Barker is implying if words mean anything. He should have qualified that statement and told the whole truth about the NIV Old Testament text. He should have listed the other things in addition to the Masoretic text that were used and not simply the Masoretic Hebrew text. Let me give you (from the 5th printing, page 29 of our *Defending the King James Bible*) 19 other things that the New International Version has used in addition to the Masoretic Hebrew text.

1. The Septuagint (LXX, the Greek Old Testament)
2. Conjecture. or no reason given
3. The Syriac Version
4. A Few Hebrew Manuscripts
5. The Latin Vulgate
6. The Dead Sea Scrolls

7. Aquila

8. The Samaritan Pentateuch

9. Quotations from Jerome

10. Josephus

11. An Ancient Hebrew scribal tradition

12. The *BIBLIA HEBRAICA* of Kittel or Stuttgartensia

13. A Variant Hebrew reading in the margin

14. Words in the Consonantal Text divided differently

15. Symmachus

16. Theodotian

17. The Targums

18. The *Juxta Hebraica* of Jerome for the Psalms

19. A Different Set of Hebrew Vowels.

Here are 19 different things used in the footnotes of the New International Version that are used to contradict the Masoretic traditional Hebrew text in the Old Testament. These things are found in my book, *Defending the King James Bible* (5th printing, pages 29-31). I urge you to get a copy of this volume. Ask your bookstore how to get it for you, or call us direct and we'll tell you how to receive it at **1-800-JOHN 10:9.** This is a falsification of the truth by Dr. Barker when he claims that his Old Testament is based on the Masoretic or Traditional Hebrew text. He should have said that 19 other things in addition to the Masoretic text were used in his NIV.

You can check this out by looking at the NIV Old Testament footnotes, and you will find every one of the above 19 items mentioned somewhere from Genesis to Malachi. If Dr. Barker were patently honest and totally above-board, he would have told the people the truth on that telecast. I am sure that Kenneth Barker knows precisely the **changes** the NIV has made in the "Masoretic Tex" but he never said so. He implied that the NIV has adhered strictly to the Old Testament "Masoretic text." The question I have is why did he not make this plain to those who listened? Is this not deceptive?

#20 Issue: Dr. Barker says his New Testament NIV text is "eclectic." (Script, p. 3)

Comment by Dr. Waite: He said in the New Testament you have an eclectic text, such as is found in the United Bible Societies' Greek text or the Nestle-Aland text. Both these have their roots in the Westcott and Hort false text of 1881. These erroneous Greek texts used by the NIV rely basically on B (Vatican) and א (Sinai) manuscripts and possibly 43 others. How could the use of 45 manuscripts out of 5,255 by any stretch of the imagination be called "eclectic"? The NIV has not taken something from all of the manuscripts at all. That's what eclectic means. " Ec" means "out from" and "lectic" comes from the Greek word, "kaleO" and means "to call." Eclectic means to "call out from," or to select from many things. Since when is that eclectic? That's almost pure B and ℵ. In using this Nestle-Aland/UBS/Westcott and Hort text, the NIV made use of less than 1% (45 manuscripts) of the Greek evidence that has been preserved for us. By the same token, the NIV has denied over 99% (5,210 manuscripts) of the evidence. This is not "eclecticism" at all.

Does God "Use and Bless" Sin?

#21 Issue: Dr. Barker gives a wrong reason for his NIV's success. He said God uses and blesses his NIV. (Script, p. 3)

Comment by Dr. Waite: God does not use things that contradict His Word. Don't drag God into the New International Version. I'm going to be very frank about this. I believe that the New International Version is one of the greatest perversions of our day. Granted, the Living Version is a greater perversion than the NIV, but the New International Version is pretty close to that. I examined closely every word of the NIV. It took 2 years and 8 months to go from Genesis to Revelation. I found over 6,653 examples of dynamic equivalency that the NIV has used. I had to quit counting because my computer was filling up and it had already taken much time. There were thousands and thousands of other examples of dynamic equivalency. Dynamic equivalency means three things: (1) adding to the Words of God; (2) subtracting from the Words of God, or (3) changing the Words of God in some other way. This research is available as **B.F.T. #1749-P** for a GIFT of **$25 + $4 P&H**. It is 284 large pages in length.

How can the God of the Bible really "bless" the New International Version which has violated His written Word by its paraphrasing? God does not contradict Himself. When God pronounces a curse upon those that add, subtract, or change His Words, that very curse is on the New International Version because they have added, subtracted, and changed His Words thousands of times. Men have taken upon themselves to change God's Words. It is not translation, but paraphrase. Notice just three of many verses:

> Deuteronomy 4:2 *"**Ye shall not add unto the word** which I command you, **neither shall ye diminish [ought] from it**, that ye may keep the commandments of the LORD your God which I command you."*
> Deuteronomy 12:32 *"What thing soever I command you, observe to do it: **thou shalt not add thereto, nor diminish from it**."*
> Proverbs 30:6 *"**Add thou not unto his words**, lest he reprove thee, and thou be found a liar."*

I do not personally believe that God can "bless" that which is in direct disobedience of His written Word!

How "Literal" Are NASV and NKJV?

#22 Issue: Dr. Barker said that the King James, the New King James, and the New American Standard used "a more literal or word-for-word approach to the translation task." (Script, p. 3)

Comment by Dr. Waite: This is not true. The New King James is not a word-for-word literal type translation as much as the King James itself is. The New American Standard Version certainly is not a "literal or word-for-word approach." I made a verse by verse analysis of the New King James compared to the Hebrew and Greek that underlies our King James Bible. I found over 2,000 examples of how the New King James added to God's Words, subtracted from God's Words, and changed God's Words. Admittedly, this is not as bad as the New International Version's 6,653. But 2,000 is 2,000 more than I'd like to see.

The New American Standard Version is not literal either. I made a verse by verse analysis of the NASV also. I found over 4,000 examples of how the New American Standard Version added to God's Words, subtracted from God's Words, and changed God's Words. How can those translations be called "literal" or "word-for-word"? The King James Bible is the only English Bible that is truly "literal" or "word-for-word" wherever possible.

NIV Is No Translation "Middle Ground"!

#23 Issue: Dr. Barker said that his NIV was a "middle ground" and a "mediating translation" between "too literal" or "too free." He said it was "middle ground" between the King James Bible and the Good News for Modern Man or the Living Version. (Script, p. 3)

Comment by Dr. Waite: The New International Versions is NOT a middle ground between the Good News Bible or Living Version and the King James Bible. The New International Version is just as free as a bird. It believes in paraphrase. It is not literal. This is why I could find 6,653 examples of adding, subtracting, or other changing of God's Words. The NIV is a long way from being a "middle ground." The New International Version is just more of the same, though admittedly not quite as bad as the Living Version.

KJB and NKJV, Same Greek Text?

#24 Issue: John Ankerberg said the New King James was based on "the same Greek text as the 1611." (Script, p. 4)

Comment by Dr. Waite: This is not completely true. I have found at least three examples of the New King James Version's use of the Westcott and Hort type of text being used in the text itself. How many other examples of non-Textus Receptus Greek text used in the top of the pages, I cannot say. It is presumed if I found three, there might be many other examples. Certainly in the footnotes of the study edition of the NKJV, there is a use of "Majority Text" citations as well as the "NU" (Nestle/United Bible Societies) text. The NKJV study edition notes in the back of the book make it clear that the editors and/or publishers do not take any stand on which text is the best--the text used on the top of the page, or the text referred to in the footnotes. This decision they leave up to their readers. They can become their own textual critics.

> **#25 Issue:** John Ankerberg brought Dr. Arthur Farstad into the picture. He is representing the New King James Version. (Script, p. 4)

Comment by Dr. Waite: At this point, Dr. Arthur Farstad is brought into the discussion. He got about 7 inches of space here. He has a lot of time for the presentation of his point, at least on this occasion. As noted above, he ranked 7th out of 9 in total number of inches in the entire Script, that is 42" out of a possible 656." This is 6% of the time which translates into only 10 minutes out of the 160 minute total.

NKJV Not Same Hebrew Text as KJB

> **#26 Issue:** Dr. Farstad said his New King James Version used the "Masoretic" Hebrew text and implied that it was the same text as that used in the King James Bible. He said "there's not much controversy about that in the Old Testament." (Script, p. 4)

Comment by Dr. Waite: Dr. Farstad implied that the Masoretic Old Testament Traditional Hebrew text of the NKJV is the identical text to that used in the King James Bible. If you read the preface of the New King James you will find that they do not use ONLY the Masoretic Traditional Hebrew. They compare and use upon occasion the readings of the following: (1) the Latin Vulgate, (2) the Septuagint, (3) ancient versions, and (4) the dead sea scrolls. [Cf. The NKJV *Preface*, p. vi]

He is also wrong when he said "there's not much controversy about that [that is, the Hebrew text] in the Old Testament." There is a whirlwind of controversy about the Hebrew text on the part of liberals, neo-evangelicals, and even so-called "Fundamentalists." The latest publication (1997) of the self-proclaimed "Fundamentalist" Central Baptist Theological Seminary in Minneapolis, Minnesota, tells a different story. In *The Bible Versions Debate*, this seminary takes the position that there are hundreds of errors in our present Masoretic Traditional Hebrew text. Dr. Roy E. Beacham, a Professor at that school, takes up various "arguments against perfect preservation in the Masoretic Text." (p. 14). He speaks repeatedly of "imperfect copies" of the Hebrew Old Testament Masoretic Text. I disagree with him completely in this view, but I cite this to show that Dr. Farstad is in error in his statement about the unity of belief on the Hebrew Old Testament Masoretic Text.

"Dynamic Equivalency"--KJB vs. Others

> **#27 Issue:** Arthur Farstad accused the King James Bible of using "dynamic equivalency" with the expression in Matthew 27:44: "They cast the same in his teeth." (Script, p. 4)

Comment by Dr. Waite: "They cast the same in his teeth," is an expression that was used in 1611 that means the same thing as "they reviled him." The word so translated is used ten times in the New Testament. In the Logos Bible Computer Program, they list "cast in the teeth" as one of the meanings of the verb used here. The main thing is that, even if you might concede this is an example here, the King James Bible does not practice dynamic equivalence as a matter of policy as do these other versions. This is an expression that was used in 1611 to convey the meaning of reproach, upbraid, or revile.

My research on Dr. Farstad's New King James Version (**B.F.T. #1442** for a GIFT of **$10+P&H**) lists **over 2,000 examples** of dynamic equivalence. This false translation technique is a **policy** of the NKJV in all of these places. My research on Dr. Wilkins' New American Standard Version (**B.F.T. #1594-P** for a GIFT of **$15+P&H**) lists **over 4,000 examples** of dynamic equivalence. My research on Dr. Barker's New International Version (**B.F.T. #1749-P** for a GIFT of **$25+P&H**) lists **over 6,653 examples** of dynamic equivalence. This indicates a definite **policy** favoring dynamic equivalence in all three of these versions, unlike the policy of the King James Bible which was both verbal and formal equivalence.

NKJV and "Dynamic Equivalency"

#28 Issue: Arthur Farstad stated of his New King James Version, "We don't ever do it [use dynamic equivalence] where it isn't needed." (Script, p. 4)

Comment by Dr. Waite: This is not true. Let's just look at a few examples. In Leviticus 8:23 (the last part) the King James Bible and the Hebrew says, "**Moses** took of the blood." What does the New King James Version say, "**He** took some of its blood." This is dynamic equivalence changing a noun to a pronoun. God said "Moses" not "he." Is Arthur Farstad tying to say that this is necessary? I found over 2,000 examples in the New King James Version, as mentioned above in **#27 Issue** where the editors added, subtracted, or changed in some other way the Words of God.

Let me give you another example. In Leviticus 8:15 (the last part of that) the King James Bible and the Hebrew both say, "**Moses** took the blood". What does the New King James Version say? In dynamic equivalent fashion it says, "**He** took the blood." It is not "he." The Hebrew says "Moses." The NKJV changes "Moses" to "he" for no good reason whatsoever. How can Arthur Farstad say that The New King James does not use dynamic equivalence "where it isn't needed"?

Rather than giving additional specific examples why don't I just give you some of the **totals** for the New King James Version. The New King James Version **ADDS** to God's Words **63 times** (adjectives, adverbs, nouns, prepositional phrases, pronouns, verbs, and miscellaneous things). It **CHANGES** God's Words **856 times** (adjectives, adverbs, clauses, interjections, nouns, phrases, plurals, prepositional phrases, prepositions, pronouns, spellings, the subject, theological terms, the verb, and miscellaneous things. It suggests the use of a non-Masoretic text in the Old Testament **48 times**. It suggests the use of a non-Textus Receptus text in the New Testament **772 times**. The New King James Version **SUBTRACTS** from God's Words **295 times** (omitting adjectives, adverbs, conjunctions, interjections, nouns, nouns for deity, prepositional phrases, pronouns, subjective mood, and verbs). I have a total of **2,034 examples** of dynamic equivalence "where it isn't needed." The evidence is all found in our **B.F.T. #1442** mentioned above.

Let's look at some examples of "adding nouns for deity." In Job 24:22, the Hebrew clearly says, "**He** draweth." In the New King James "he" is changed to "God" in "**God** draws." They are adding God's name when God's name is not in the Hebrew. Is that dynamic equivalence "needed"? Is that necessary or needful to add God's name when God is not there? No, this is an error. Let me give you another example. In Acts 7:5 the Greek clearly says, "**He** gave him". What does the New King James Version say, "**God** gave him." "God" is not there in Acts 7:5. There is no manuscript that has "God" in it, but the NKJV adds this word. The NASV and the NIV do not add God's Name in this verse. The NKJV is even worse then the other two at this point!

The same in Lamentations 3:28 where the Hebrew clearly says, "**He** hath borne." The New King James Version says, "**God** has laid," adding God's name where it isn't there. Look at Job 9:4 where the Hebrew clearly says, "**He** is wise." The New King James say "**God** is wise." This is error. "God" or "Elohim" is not there. As in Acts 7:5 above, the NASV and the NIV do not add God's Name in this verse. Again, the NKJV is even worse than the other two at this point! The same is found in Job 15:15, where the Hebrew and the King James Bible both say, "**He** putteth no trust." The New King James says, "**God** puts no trust." The NKJV adds the Name of deity, "God." This is "taking the name of the Lord thy God in vain" (Exodus 20:7; Deuteronomy 5:11) as far as I'm concerned. The same in Romans 3:29. The King James Bible says, "Not also of the Gentiles." The New King James says, "Not also the **God** of the Gentiles." This is adding the name of God where it does not belong.

Is Dr. Farstad's statement true or false when he said: **"We don't ever do it [use dynamic equivalence] where it isn't needed"**? Is it "needed" to add the Name of God when the Name of Deity is not in the Hebrew or Greek texts? I do not believe that it is. It is forbidden by God Himself to **ADD** to His Words!

KJB Minutes--In Latin, or English?

#29 Issue: Arthur Farstad stated of the meetings of the King James Bible translators, "The meetings, the journal meetings were taken in Latin. They spoke in English but the notes were in Latin." (Script, p. 5)

Comment by Dr. Waite: I have what remains of John Bois' notes that he took of the final revising committee's work on the 1611 King James Bible. He was the secretary of the 1611 translation committee. The notes are in English with only a few citations from Latin. If you would like a copy of these note you can get them from The Bible for Today. The book is **B.F.T.** #2326 for a GIFT to **B.F.T.** of $22.00. These are the only notes that remain of the 1611 translation committee. I do not know where Dr. Farstad got his mistaken belief that "**the notes were in Latin**" when, in fact, the only notes of the secretary, John Bois, that remain (after having been lost for 300 years) are in English.

What % of Greek Texts Are Same for All?

#30 Issue: Kenneth Barker said: "All translations today translate the same Greek text over 98 percent of the time. That is a fact. It's been well documented by Dan [Wallace], and by others." (Script, p. 5)

Comment by Dr. Waite: This is a false statement. What they're saying is the Greek text of the New Testament that underlies our King James Bible is almost the same as the Greek text that underlies the new perversions of the New Testament. By their use of "over 98 percent" which means "less than 2 percent," they are saying the differences are so slight that you shouldn't even talk about them, much less worry about them.

Let me give you some statistics. In my book, *Defending The King James Bible*, look in the *Foreword*, (page xii, 5th printing). You will see a chart that shows that the Textus Receptus has 140,521 Greek words. The Westcott and Hort text (and for all practical purposes also the Nestle/Aland and United Bible Societies text) changes the Textus Receptus that underlies the King James Bible in 5,604 places in the New Testament. Those changes include 9,970 Greek words. The 9,970 Greek words could mean adding, subtracting, or changing the Greek words. This is 15.4 Greek words per page on the average. This is a change of **7%** of the Greek words one way or another. This means that these two Greek texts agree only **93%** of the time **not "less than 98% of the time."** If you put all of the changes that they have made in these new versions (at least in the Westcott and Hort Greek text which is basically follow today) on consecutive pages, you would come up with 45.9 pages of differences in the Greek New Testament between the Westcott and Hort Greek text and that of the Textus Receptus. These statistics were derived from my own personal counting of the 5,604 places in the Westcott and Hort Greek text which differed from the Textus Receptus. I used Dr. Frederick Scrivener's *Greek New Testament* which indicated the Westcott and Hort changes in **bold type face**. I arrived at the 9,970 Greek words that differed in some way by counting the number of words in the Dr. Scrivener's footnotes that Westcott and Hort inserted or subtracted or changed in some other way from the Textus Receptus readings. Dr. Scrivener's text is available as **B.F.T.** #1670 for a GIFT of **$35+P&H**. The reader is invited to count the words for himself to ascertain if 5,604 and 9,970 are correct figures.

How can Dr. Kenneth Barker say that all translations today translate the same Greek text over 98 percent of the time? If you subtract 7% from 100% you get 93%, not 98%. What Kenneth Barker is trying to get you to believe is that the New International Greek text is just about the same as the Textus Receptus Greek text that underlies the King James Bible. This is grossly misleading! This type of error cannot go unchallenged. It is important to set the record straight on this false statement by the NIV's Kenneth Barker that went out over this telecast that went out all over the United States and on the videos as well.

Are Doctrines Different in the Versions?

#31 Issue: Kenneth Barker said: "The differences, then, make up only less than 2 percent of the total text of the New Testament and no basic Christian doctrine hinges on that less than 2 percent." (Script, p. 5)

Comment by Dr. Waite: That is another serious falsehood by Dr. Barker. In my book, *Defending The King James Bible*, in chapter 5, I enumerate 158 theological errors and heresies that come from the NIV's B and ℵ Greek text, and the NIV English translation. Many of these, I think you would agree, are "basic Christian doctrine." These 158 are only some of the total of 356 doctrinal errors in the Greek text of Westcott and Hort and the consequent English translation of the NIV. These 356 doctrinal errors of the text and translations are enumerated, every one, by Dr. Jack Moorman in his excellent book, *The Early Manuscripts and the Authorized Version--A Closer Look.* (It is **B.F.T. #1825** for a GIFT of **$15+P&H**).

These doctrinal heresies include not only Kenneth Barker's New International Version, but also the New American Standard Version, the New King James Version in the footnotes, and the New Berkeley Version. The four versions named above are versions that many Bible believing Christians are using today. The list could also include the apostate-type versions such as the Revised Standard Version, the New Revised Standard Version, and others. I was principally interested in the versions that Bible believing Christians were using.

In Chapter 5 of the book, I have quotations of at least 8 Christian leaders who insist that no basic Christian doctrine is involved in either the English versions or the Greek text from which they come. I have written a later volume, entitled: *Patterns for Overhead Transparencies Defending the King James Bible.* This is available as **B.F.T. #2536** (240 large pages) for a GIFT of **$24+P&H**. On pages 189-195, I have added Kenneth Barker's name along with 5 other Christian leaders making a total of 14 Christian leaders, past and present, who falsely deny that doctrine is involved in the Greek texts or in any of the English versions.

As we have previously pointed out, the percentage difference is not 2%, but 7%. There are a total of 356 doctrinal passages that **do** differ between the Textus Receptus Greek New Testament and the Westcott and Hort Greek New Testament. Dr. Jack Moorman has spelled out 356 doctrinal passages where the two Greek texts **do** differ. For Dr. Kenneth Barker to say that "no basic Christian doctrine hinges on that less than 2%" is indeed false. Basic doctrine **IS** changed!

For example, the King James Bible agrees with the Textus Receptus and says:

> John 6:47, *"Verily, verily I say unto thee,* **he that believeth <u>on me</u>** *hath everlasting life."* (KJB)

This is sound doctrine. Only through the Lord Jesus Christ can everlasting life be received.

On the other hand, the New International Greek text, and the New American Standard Greek text are both heretical in this verse. So are both the NASV and the NIV. Notice the heresy and false doctrine they teach in this verse:

> John 6:47 *"Truly, truly, I say to you,* **he who believes** *has eternal life."* (NASB)

> John 6:47 *"I tell you the truth,* **he who believes** *has everlasting life."* (NIV)

This is a "basic" **doctrinal** and a **theological** difference. One says you just believe and you have everlasting life. One says you have to believe on the Lord Jesus Christ. This is how we are saved by trusting in the Lord Jesus Christ and Him alone. Kenneth Barker's statement is absolutely false both as to the percentage of difference and as to basic doctrines not being involved!

#32 Issue: Dan Wallace, a Teacher at Dallas Theological Seminary, said: "This, again, is what Ken [Barker] pointed out in that <u>no major doctrines, in fact, no essential doctrines have been affected by any of these variants</u>. . . ." As noted above, Dan Wallace ranked 3rd out of 9 in total number of inches in the entire Script, that is 88" out of a possible 656." This is 14% of the time which translates into 22 minutes out of the 160 minute total. (Script, pp. 5-6)

Comment by Dr. Waite: This is completely false. Here are some other men who nevertheless agree with Dan Wallace on this point, though in error.

1.   Westcott and Hort falsely stated in their *Introduction to the Greek New Testament*, page 282:

> *"There are no deliberate falsifications of the text for dogmatic purposes."*

In other words they are saying there are no doctrines that have been changed. They agree with Dan Wallace, but they are in error.

2.   Dr. Arthur T. Pierson falsely stated:

> *"Not one of these differences affects a single vital doctrine of the Word of God."*

3.   Dr. Louis T. Talbot falsely stated:

> *"No fundamental doctrine has been changed in the least by the later version."*

4.   Dr. John R. Rice falsely stated:

> *"The differences in the translations are so minor, so insignificant, that*

we can be sure not a single doctrine, not a single statement of fact, not a single command or exhortation, has been missed in our translations."

5. Dr. Robert L. Sumner falsely stated:,
    " The rare parts about which there is still uncertainty do not effect [sic] in any way any doctrine."

6. Dr. Robert L. Thomas falsely stated:
    "And no major doctrine of scripture is affected by a variant reading."

7. Dr. H. S. Miller falsely stated:
    "These variations include such matters as differences in spelling . . . no doctrine is affected."

8. Dr. Stanley Gundry falsely stated:
    "Only a few outstanding problems remain, and these do not affect doctrine or divine command to us."

9. Dr. Ernest D Pickering falsely stated:
    "Important differences of textual readings are relatively few and almost none would affect any major Christian doctrine."

10. Rev. Richard DeHaan from Radio Bible Class falsely stated:
    "Not one of them involves a single basic doctrine of the Christian faith. None of the thousand of variants denies one foundational Christian truth."

11. Bob Jones Jr. (Chancellor of Bob Jones University) falsely stated:
    "There is no theological difference. The choice of manuscripts is not a choice of orthodoxy versus heterodoxy; it is a matter of which of the orthodox manuscripts a translator wishes to use."

12. John Ankerberg on one of his programs falsely stated:
    "Leaving Christians with only a bias and distorted text that is seriously compromised doctrinally, but in a good conservative translation none of these charges can be substantiated."

13. Dr. Kenneth Barker falsely stated:
    ". . . No basic Christian doctrine hinges on that less than 2 percent."

14. Dr. Dan Wallace falsely stated:
    "No essential doctrines have been affected by any of these variants."

In other words there is no compromise doctrinally. These quotations in full are found in *Patterns for Overhead Transparencies Defending the King James Bible* as mentioned above, pages 188-195.

Could all of the above-named men and their various writings be wrong? Yes, indeed, every last one of them, and all the many others who have been making such false statements for decades are all wrong! Let's take a look at some of the doctrines and theological verities that are involved. All of them prove these preceding writers to be in error.

In I Corinthians 15:47, the Textus Receptus and the King James Bible say: "The first man is the earth earthy, the second man is **the Lord** from Heaven." These other manuscripts: B and א, plus the New International, New American Standard Version, and New King James version in the footnotes, take away **the Lord** from Heaven. They say he's merely "from heaven," but He is not the "**LORD**" from heaven. Is this not doctrine?

In I Timothy 3:16 the Textus Receptus and the King James Bible say: "Great is the mystery of godliness **God** was manifest in the flesh. . . ." There is nothing more essential than this doctrine of the Incarnation of Christ found in I Timothy 3:16, but the New International Version does not have **God** manifest in the flesh at all. It has: "**He** appeared in a body." The same with the New American Standard, the New King James in the footnotes, and the New Berkeley. They have taken away the fact that "Theos" (God) was manifest in the flesh. That's basic, cardinal, vital doctrine!

In 1 John 4:3 the Textus Receptus and the King James Bible say: "Every spirit that confesseth not that Jesus **Christ is come in the flesh** is not of God." These other versions take away the words, "**Christ is come in the flesh**" and they make it simply, "Anyone that confesses not Jesus is not of God." B has taken this clause away. So has the New American Standard. That is certainly doctrine, is it not?

In Matthew 18:11 the Textus Receptus and the King James Bible say: "**For the Son of Man is come to save that which was lost**." That whole verse is eliminated from the New International Version. It is put in the brackets of doubt in the New American Standard. It is suggested that it be eliminated in the footnotes of the New King James. That's doctrine is it not?

In John 7:8 the Textus Receptus and the King James Bible say: "Go ye up unto this feast. **I go not up yet unto this feast** for my time has not yet full come." א (the Sinai manuscript) takes away the word "yet," so the New American Standard Version simply says, "**I do not go up to this feast** because My time has not yet full come." They take away the word "**yet**" (and the New King James in the footnotes takes away that word "yet"). The Lord Jesus Christ was speaking to his half brothers. The Lord Jesus DID go up as is mentioned in the next few verses. The false Greek text and the NASV have the Lord Jesus Christ being a LIAR! Is this not vital and basic doctrine on the Person of Christ?

What about the power of Christ to create all things. In Ephesians 3:9 the Textus Receptus and the King James Bible say, "And to make all {men} see what {is} the fellowship of the mystery, which from the beginning of the world hath been hid in God, who created all things **by Jesus Christ**." B and א take away the words, "**by Jesus Christ**." The New Berkeley, the New International, the New American Standard, and the New King James in the footnotes also take away these words. They simply say "created all things" and take away the part that Jesus Christ had in creation. Is this not vital, basic Christian doctrine?

We've got 158 of these doctrinal passages that are involved. Let's go to a simple one. John 3:15, "That whosoever believeth in Him **should not perish**, but have eternal life." The Vatican (B), the Sinai (ℵ), the New International Version, the New American Standard Version, and the New King James in the footnotes all take away those three little words, "**should not perish**." This takes away Hell, punishment, and eternal doom right out of John 3:15. Here are these men on this telecast who are telling you that there is no doctrine affected by any of these variants. You can see that this is not the case, can you not?

The Deity of Christ

#33 Issue: Dan Wallace also said: "'Gee, is the Deity of Christ found in the NIV and the NAS? Is it found in the New King James? Is it found in the old King James?' Sure is. <u>Found everywhere</u> in there." (Script, p. 6)

Comment by Dr. Waite: That is a false statement. The Deity of the Lord Jesus Christ is not found everywhere that it should be found in the New International Version. The same is true for the New American Standard Version and the New King James Version's footnotes. It **IS** found, however, EVERYWHERE it should be found in the King James Bible.

II.
COMMENTS ON PROGRAM #2
Script, Pages 6-12

Mr. James White

> **#34 Issue:** Program #2 begins with an extensive comment from James White who has written a book on *The King James Only Controversy.* (Script, pp. 6-7)

Comment by Dr. Waite: In program #2 James White seems to be conducting a non-stop filibuster. I don't know why he was on the program. James White is not one of the authors of the New King James, the New American Standard, or the New International Version. James White has a total of 21 inches of space of talk in Program #2. It appears that nothing of significance is being discussed. One reason is the fact that there are **nine** people on the program, all trying to talk at once. When so many people talk they leave out facts. As noted above, James White ranks 2nd out of 9 in total number of inches in the entire Script, that is 112" out of a possible 656." This is 17% of the time which translates into 27 minutes out of the 160 minute total. He talked the longest of any of the other participants. Only the host out-talked him.

Apostles and Prophets not "Inspired"

> **#35 Issue:** John Ankerberg turned the microphone over to James White and asked him how we got the Bible. James White said: "It's an amazing act of grace that God has deemed it proper to communicate with man who gave His Word to __INSPIRED prophets and apostles.__" (Script, p. 6)

Comment by Dr. Waite: This is a theological error. There is not a single prophet or apostle who was "inspired." The word "inspired" in the New Testament (2 Timothy 3:16) means "God-breathed." How could men be somehow "breathed out" by God? It's the inspired Words, not the "inspired prophets," not the "inspired apostles." 2 Timothy 3:16 says: "All Scripture is given by inspiration of God." This is the only time that the word "inspiration" is used in the New Testament. It's the word "*theopneustos.*" It comes from two Greek words, "*theos*" (God) and "*pneO*" (to breathe.) It means "God-breathed." What was it that "God-breathed"? It was "*pasa graphE*" (all scripture). It's the "*graphE*" or the Scripture, the Words that are "God-breathed." God breathed out the words. He did not inspire or breathe out prophets or apostles. This is a theological error on James White's part.

In our Dean Burgon Society's *Articles of Faith* we say:

> "*We believe in the plenary, verbal, divine inspiration of the sixty-six canonical books* [notice the inspiration of the books, not of the prophets or apostles] *of the Old and New Testaments from Genesis to Revelation in their original languages, and in their consequent infallibility and inerrancy in all matters in which they speak. (2 Timothy 3:16-17; 2 Peter 1:21; 1 Thessalonians 2:13). The books known as the Apocrypha, however, are not the inspired Word of God in any sense whatsoever. As the Bible uses it, the term "inspiration" refers to the writings, not the writers (2 Timothy 3:16,17). The writers are spoken of as being "holy men of God" who were "moved," "carried," or "borne" along by the Holy Spirit (2 Peter 1:21) in such a definite way that their writings* [notice not themselves, but their writings] *were supernaturally, plenarily, and verbally inspired, free from any error, infallible and inerrant as no other writings have ever been or ever will be inspired.*"

Now, that's the definition of "inspired" and what is inspired and what isn't inspired. Mr. James White should know that. He has written a whole book ridiculing the people who stand for the King James Bible, the Textus Receptus (the Greek text which underlies it), and the Masoretic Hebrew text (which underlies the Old Testament). Here he makes this big theological blunder right off the bat talking about "inspired prophets and apostles." This criticism of Mr. White is not being overly "technical." This is simple theology. Could his failure to understand this truth indicates that Mr. White has a very basic flaw in his theological preparation at Fuller Theological Seminary and other schools he attended?

#36 Issue: James White said of the apostles and prophets: "They wrote letters to churches." (Script, p. 6)

Comment by Dr. Waite: Why do we say that the apostles and prophets were not "inspired"? If they were inspired, everything that they spoke at any time (not only what was in Scripture) would be inspired. For instance, Catholic doctrine teaches that when the Pope is supposed to be speaking *ex cathedra* his words are infallible and perfect. We know that the Pope is not speaking *ex cathedra* in any way. In other words we don't believe that the Pope is either infallible or perfect at any time. If the "apostles and prophets" were "inspired," then everything the prophets and apostles said and did would be "inspired" or infallible and perfect. This would be serious error. It was only what the prophets wrote down in Scripture that was inspired or God-breathed. ("All **Scripture** is **given by inspiration of God.** . ." 2 Timothy 3:16). That which was "given by inspiration" was "Scripture." The word for "Scripture" is *graphE* which means, "that which is written down." Since the "apostles and prophets" were not "written down," they could not be "inspired" according to 2 Timothy 3:16.

Roman Empire's Destruction of Bibles

#37 Issue: James White told about the Roman persecution of the Christians. (Script, p. 6)

Comment by Dr. Waite: It is a fact that the Roman persecutors killed the Christians. They would take the Bibles that the Christians had in their hands and burn them. This is one reason that we say the Scriptures upon which our King James Bible is based were of more recent date. We believe the exemplars, the original exemplars, after they were copied exactly, were buried so heretics could not pervert them to conform to their heresies. During the Diocletian persecution, the Bibles were burned along with the people who owned them. The false Scriptures that Mr. James White believes are the Scriptures to use are the Westcott and Hort type of texts or the B and ℵ type of texts. Mr. White says these types of texts were buried in the sands of Egypt. They were Egyptian texts. That's important to see. These Egyptian texts were false texts.

These were the false texts that the churches never followed because they knew they were erroneous. The originals were not in Egypt. There was not a single letter that was ever written to the church in Egypt. Letters were written to the church at Thessalonica, to the church at Ephesus, to the church at Colosse, and so on, but not to the church in Egypt. That is why those old manuscripts B (the Vatican which was found in the Vatican library) and ℵ(which was found in St. Catherine's Convent and was about to be burned) had survived. B and ℵ were hidden away and not used. Because these copies were not used they were more easily preserved by the favorable, dry Egyptian climate. Some of the older and accurate Scriptures of the Traditional Text and Textus Receptus variety which were used repeatedly, were destroyed by the persecutors of Rome. Others of the older and accurate Scriptures, after they were exactly and correctly copied, were reverently buried by the Christians. They did not want the heretics to get hold of these exemplars thus making it possible to distort them to go along with their heresies, and pass them off as "originals."

Are New Testament Copies Sloppy?

#38 Issue: James White implied that the copyists made many errors at the first. (Script, p. 6)

Comment by Dr. Waite: Here Mr. White is trying to show that the Christians made sloppy copies in the original times, and that they didn't really copy them accurately. I believe that is far from the truth. These Christians revered the very Words of the Living God. They believed the Scriptures were inspired of God. The copyists wanted to be just as meticulous as the scribes were when they copied the Old Testament Hebrew text.

Erasmus Attacked by James White

#39 Issue: James White talked about "humanists" such as Desiderius Erasmus who were interested in the original languages of the Bible. (Script, p. 7)

Comment by Dr. Waite: Though James White said that the "humanists" of that day were different from those of today, it should be emphasized again. Erasmus was not a "secular humanist" as those today, but merely one who tried to further humane pursuits.

#40 Issue: James White said "Erasmus was working with a very small number of manuscripts . . ." (Script, p. 7)

Comment by Dr. Waite: First of all, Erasmus was not the one who originated the text which he used. The text that Erasmus used descended from the originals of Paul and Peter and John and James and all the different apostles who wrote the Words of God. Dean John William Burgon referred to this type of text as the Traditional Text. We call it today, the Textus Receptus or Received Text. By the way, the Dean Burgon Society, as of this writing, has reprinted two of Dean Burgon's books. The first is *The Last Twelve Verses of Mark* (**B.F.T. #1139**, 400 pages, perfect bound @ **$15.00 + $4 P&H**). The second is *The Revision Revised* (**B.F.T. #611**, 640 pages, hardback @ **$25.00 + $5 P&H**). You should also get our book, *Defending the King James Bible* (**B.F.T. #1594-P**, 352 pages, hardback @ **$12.00 + $4 P&H**). Two other books by Dean Burgon (now in copy format) are scheduled for reprinting by the Dean Burgon Society also in early 1997. They are *The Traditional Text* (**B.F.T. #1159**, @ **$15.00+$4 P&H**) and *The Causes of Corruption* (**B.F.T. #1160** @ **$15.00+P&H**). Secondly, Mr James White said that Erasmus operated from a very small number of manuscripts. Erasmus was like these pollsters that go around at election time. They sample opinion. From these samples we have the results (40% for this candidate, 50% for this candidate, and 10% for this candidate, and so on) according to the presumably representative polls. This is exactly what Erasmus did. He took a sample of all the Greek texts that were available. He knew about B and ℵ, the Vatican and Sinai manuscripts. These are the false Greek texts copied by Egyptian heretics--the new age men, the Platonists, the neo-Platonists, and the Gnostics. Erasmus rejected all of them. So, when James White says that Erasmus took just a few, you must remember that these were samples and they were of a particular type of Greek manuscript. What was that particular type of Greek manuscript? That was the manuscript sample that represented the text that underlies our King James Bible. It's called the Traditional Greek text or the Textus Receptus.

Do you know how many manuscripts follow or go along with Erasmus' Greek text today? His sampling was correct. There are 5,255 total Greek manuscripts as of 1967 (by Kurt Aland) that have been preserved for us in the Greek language. Do you know how many of those that we find follow the Textus Receptus which underlies our King James Bible? Over 99% of that total number, or 5,210 follow our Textus Receptus. Do you know how many Greek manuscripts go along with these versions that these men are trying to push on this program? Less than 1% of the evidence. There are approximately 45 manuscripts that go along with these false text--B and ℵ, and 43 of their allies.

Is Textus Receptus Limited to One Area?

#41 Issue: James White said the Textus Receptus "comes from the Byzantine Family." (Script, p. 7)

Comment by Dr. Waite: James White says that this text is going to come from a geographical area and that we have a certain type of text coming from a certain type of area. Let's just quote a few things from Dean John William Burgon's book *The Last Twelve Verses of Mark.* Look on page 37:

> *"In the second century Irenaeus, the Peshitto, and the Italic Version plainly attests that in Gaul, in Mesopotamia, the African Province the same verses (Mark 16:9-20) were unhesitatingly received within a century (more or less) of the date of the inspired autograph of the evangelist himself (Mark)."*

So, you can see there was a wide variety of places where these words arose. For instance in the third century, you have the testimony and statements in favor of Mark 16:9-20. The manuscript evidence has entirely forsaken us, there were no manuscripts in the 3rd century (B and ℵ weren't around). We find Hippolytus, the Curetonian Syriac Version, and the Thebaic Version bearing plain testimony that in that early period in at least three different provinces of primitive Christendom there was no suspicion whatsoever attached to these verses (Mark 16:9-20)

What I am saying is there were churches in vast areas of Christendom that used Mark 16:9-20. It is false to say that there was just one same text (the Textus Receptus) that came from one particular region. That is plainly false. As for these versions that are translations from the early Greek texts, Dean Burgon says on page 36:

> *"For these versions not so much show what individuals held as what churches have believed and taught concerning the sacred text." (op. cit.,* p. 36)

Now notice these churches are mighty churches in Syria, Mesopotamia, the African provinces, Italy, Palestine, and Egypt. In other words, there were many early churches from a wide area of the world that used the text that underlies our King James Bible. It is false to say that the Textus Receptus manuscripts came from only one corner of the then-known world. It came from every area of Christendom and not just the Byzantine area.

The Heretics' Knives on the Greek Texts

#42 Issue: James White said that the Textus Receptus was longer than the Westcott-Hort type of text. He said the T.R. "text exhibits what's called a fuller flavor." He said this in a disparaging manner. (Script, p. 7)

Comment by Dr. Waite: What he should say is that those false texts that he and the New International and New American Standard worship (B and ℵ--the Vatican and Sinai) exhibit a shorter text. The Textus Receptus was shortened by the heretics' knives by a total of 2,886 Greek words. The words were actually counted chapter by chapter by Dr. Jack Moorman in his book, *Missing in Modern Versions--Is the Full Truth Being Told?* [It is **B.F.T. #1726** @ $8.00 + $4 P&H] Did you know that? My friend, the fuller text is the real text. The text that James White, the New International Version, the New American Standard Version, the New King James Version (in the footnotes of the study edition) is the false text which has been shortened by 2,886 Greek words. Do you know why this was done and by whom? It was done in large measure by the various Gnostic and other heretics because they did not like the truth that was contained in these various words. In Dean Burgon's book, *The Causes of Corruption,* (**B.F.T. #1160**) in Chapter 13, on page 192 he says,

> "*It is even notorious that in the earliest age of all the New Testament Scriptures were subjected to such influence* [changes or cutting away of words] *in the age that immediately succeeded the apostolic* [within 100 years after the Bible was written] *there were heretical teachers not a few where, finding their tenants refuted by the plain Word of God, they bent themselves against the written Word with all their power. From seeking to evacuate its teaching it was a single step to falsify its testimony.*"

One of the ways of "falsifying its testimony" was to shorten the text by 2,886 Greek words. Because of this shortening, and for other reasons, there are a total of 356 doctrinal passages that are in error in the B and ℵ type of Greek texts. In these same 356 passages, the Textus Receptus is doctrinally correct.

The Title of the Lord Jesus Christ

#43 Issue: James White thought there was little difference in the title "Jesus" or "Lord Jesus Christ." He told a lady that he thought there was no problem with shortening His title. (Script, p. 7)

Comment by Dr. Waite: The "Lord Jesus Christ" is the title of our Savior and for James White to pass off this lady who prefers the entire title of the "Lord Jesus Christ" is wrong. Do you realize that the apostates and modernists refer to the Lord Jesus Christ as simply "Jesus"? The modernists prefer "Jesus" because they don't believe in His Deity. They don't believe He is Lord or

"Kurios," absolute Deity, God the Son and the Son of God--the Son of God from all eternity past. They don't believe that He is the Messiah or the Christ of God. They like the name "Jesus" which means "Savior," but they just think that this is His human name and not that He is Deity, God in the flesh.

James White is trying at this juncture to head off the strong documentary facts that the New International Version and the New American Standard Version are shorter than the King James Bible in many places. This is true also when referring to the titles of the Lord Jesus Christ. What did Paul say in Acts 16:30-31 when the Phillipian jailor asked, "What must I do to be saved?" Paul said, "Believe on the **Lord Jesus Christ** and thou shalt be saved and thy house." This is the full title of Jesus and this is the title that Paul used. I realize that in Scripture Jesus' shorter title is used like in Matthew 1:21 (and in other places): "Thou shalt call his name **Jesus,** for he shall save his people from their sins." The King James Bible does not use this shorter title at all times. But when the Textus Receptus uses His full title, it should not be shortened for any reason.

The Fallacy of "Text Families"

#44 Issue: James White said: "as we compare the text families." (Script, p. 7)

Comment by Dr. Waite: Neither Dean Burgon nor his close associate, Rev. Edward Miller, believed that there were such things as "text families." Textual families were a concoction of Fenton John Anthony Hort and Bishop Brooke Foss Westcott as they expressed it in their *Introduction of the Greek New Testament* of 1881. They had to devise the so-called "text families" in order to put down and defeat the Textus Receptus which contains the greatest number of manuscripts in existence today--about 5,210 or over 99% of the 5,255 manuscripts as of 1967. This erroneous concept of "text families" was a plan to defeat the 99% of the manuscripts compared with the less than 1% on which the Greek texts of Westcott and Hort, Nestle-Aland, United Bible Societies, Souter and others are founded.

In order to overturn the huge numbers of the Textus Receptus manuscripts that underlie our King James Bible, Westcott and Hort had to invent the concept of "text families." They made up four "text families." They called the Textus Receptus (1) the Byzantine Family. They also had three other "families": (2) a Western Family, (3) a Caesarean Family, and (4) an Alexandrian Family. They divided those three "text families" up among the approximate 45 manuscripts that belong to them. The Textus Receptus, or the so-called Byzantine Family, has approximately 5,210 members in it. In effect, Westcott and Hort, and others who follow their false documentation and reasoning today, say that each "text family" only has one vote. In this way, they were able to manipulate a 3 to 1 vote in favor of their false Greek texts and against the Textus Receptus in many portions of the Greek New Testament. This is a false notion. In reality, there are no such thing as "text families."

    Dean Burgon had an illustration which I think is interesting. He said that the idea of text families, that is that one manuscript is related to another, is foolish. In only one or two instances he felt that this might be the case, but basically it is like going into a cemetery of unmarked graves. Since they are unmarked, it is impossible to tell which grave (if any) is occupied by a person in the "family" or related to a person in another grave. So it is with the Greek manuscripts. These manuscripts are like orphan children who have lost their parents. None can tell for certain who is related to whom.

The Pride of the "Christian Scholars"

> **#45 Issue:** James White said: "we, as Christian scholars today."
> (Script, p. 7)

    Comment by Dr. Waite: James White considers himself a scholar. This is interesting. John Ankerberg had on his telecast the editor of the New International Version, the editor of the New American Standard Version, and the editor of the New King James Version, along with others. James White includes himself as a "Christian scholar." I don't think he is very scholarly to call the Lord Jesus Christ just "Jesus." I don't think he is very scholarly to call the prophets and apostles "inspired" instead of the Words of God. Inspiration refers to words and not men. Such boasting on Mr. White's part sounded strange, and certainly anything but humble. I wonder what how he defines the term, "scholar"?

Which Bible Has God "Preserved"?

> **#46 Issue:** James White said, "God has preserved His Word for us in a miraculous way." (Script, p. 7)

    Comment by Dr. Waite: The question is what "Word" or what "Words" has God preserved for us and where has He preserved it. This is where we would differ with Mr. James White and four or five of the other men on this television panel (John Ankerberg included). These of the "critical text" position believe that God has preserved His Word in the Greek New Testament in the basic Westcott and Hort type of shorter text. This text is 2,886 words shorter than the Textus Receptus Greek text that underlies our King James Bible. I believe that God has preserved His Word in the Textus Receptus Greek text, the Received Text, that underlies our King James Bible. In the English language, I believe God has preserved His Word in the King James Bible because it alone, of all of the various English versions, translates accurately all of the proper Hebrew Words and all of the proper Greek Words in the Old and New Testaments. This cannot be said of the New International Version, the New American Standard Version, the New King James Version, or any other of the English versions because of their false texts and their false techniques of translation..

#47 Issue: John Ankerberg then made unsubstantiated comments in criticizing the New Testament "scribes." (Script, p. 7)

Comment by Dr. Waite: John Ankerberg is making this up. There is no indication concerning the details when "letters and books" of the "original" writings were copied such as how many of them were careful and how many were not. They were all careful. How does he know that "some were not too smart" and other things he stated about them? There is no documentation offered for proof of these comments. He doesn't even know who all the "scribes" were, much less their intelligence or scribal habits.

Psalm 12:7--Hebrew & Greek, or KJB?

#48 Issue: Though he said he doesn't claim "inspiration" for the King James Version, Dr. Gipp said "the King James Bible is a fulfillment of Psalm 12:7." (Script, p. 7)

Comment by Dr. Waite: I'm glad that he doesn't claim inspiration of the King James Bible as Dr. Peter Ruckman has done. When he claims that the King James Bible is a fulfillment of Psalm 12:7, this is not correct." When God promised to preserve His Words, those "PRESERVED WORDS" are in the languages of Hebrew, Greek, and a few verses of Aramaic. This does not include English, Spanish, French, German, the Russian, Chinese, Japanese, Italian, or any other language. God wants us to translate accurately His Hebrew/Aramaic and Greek Words into all of these languages, but God did not promise to "preserve" His Words in all those languages because He didn't give them to us in those languages in the first place. You cannot "preserve" what has not already been in existence. His Words that He promised to preserve and has preserved are His Hebrew and Greek Words from the Old and New Testament. From those original words we must have faithful translations into all the languages of the world.

#49 Issue: Dr. Gipp quoted Psalm 12:6-7. He then said "And so God said He would preserve them." (Script, p. 7)

Comment by Dr. Waite: In Psalm 12:6-7, the "them" in the phrases "keep them" and "preserve them" refers to the Hebrew and Greek Words, not to the English or any other foreign language. I believe the King James Bible "preserves" the Hebrew and Greek words that have been "Preserved" for us in that it translates accurately into English every Hebrew and every Greek word that were in the originals. It is a lower case "p" for the KJB and an upper case "P" for the Hebrew/Aramaic and Greek original language texts. There is an important distinction between these two concepts and definitions of preservation.

#50 Issue: Samuel Gipp sought to apply this language to the English King James Bible. (Script, pp. 7-8)

Comment by Dr. Waite: Samuel Gipp is again trying to say that the King James Bible is the Bible to which Psalm 12:6-7 is referring. I do not agree with this. The English language was not even on this earth when that Psalm was written. How could it refer to English? These are the kinds of erroneous and unthinking remarks that cause people to criticize all of us who defend the King James Bible. We must be very careful in how we interpret verses in God's Word.

Dr. Strouse Interrupted

> **#51 Issue:** Dr. Strouse could only say: "I think they had the Byzantine Text or the Traditional Text...." Dan Wallace interrupted him. (Script, p. 8)

Comment by Dr. Waite: Dr. Strouse is trying to get in here to speak, but the others won't let him. James White has had 2 big full printed columns of 22 inches total so far, and here Dr. Strouse has only a one liner. They interrupted him and won't let him speak his mind. I think this is most unfair.

Byzantine vs. Textus Receptus & KJB

> **#52 Issue:** Dan Wallace said: "Okay, but the Byzantine Text is not identical with the King James, it is not identical with the TR (Textus Receptus)." (Script, p. 8)

Comment by Dr. Waite: Here is Dan Wallace implying that the Byzantine text or the Traditional text is not identical with the Textus Receptus and does not go along with the King James Bible. This is misleading. 99% of the evidence goes along with the text of the King James Bible. They won't let Dr. Strouse talk about this.

> **#53 Issue:** Dan Wallace stated, of the Traditional Text, "There are at least six to ten variations per chapter for even the closest two manuscripts that we have." (Script, p. 8)

Comment by Dr. Waite: "Six to ten variations **per chapter**?" I really don't know where Dan Wallace gets his figures. I am dead certain that he has not personally examined every one of the 5,210 Greek manuscripts of the Textus Receptus variety (over 99% of the evidence), nor has any other living or dead human being! Most of these variations are spelling. In any event, this is a very tiny number compared to the differences to be found in the manuscripts of the Westcott and Hort Greek type of texts such as B (Vatican) and ℵ (Sinai). It is also small compared to the Westcott and Hort Greek text changes from the Textus Receptus. The Westcott and Hort text changed the Textus Receptus in 5,604 places (by my actual count). This is an average of 15.9 Greek words **per page** instead of six to ten variation per chapter.

> **#54 Issue:** Samuel Gipp said the other versions would "lose" if

compared to the King James Bible. (Script, p. 8)

> **Comment by Dr. Waite:** I agree with that. These other versions are extremely defective. (Script, p. 9)

Which Version Is Most Accurate?

> **#55 Issue:** John Ankerberg asked Dan Wallace: "Which English translation that you've got at home there is the most accurate?" (Script, p. 9)

> **Comment by Dr. Waite:** Which Bible is the most accurate? I have analyzed the New King James Version and have found over 2,000 additions, subtractions, or changes of God's Words. I have analyzed the New American Standard Version and have found over 4,000 places where it has departed from the Hebrew and Greek. The New International Version has departed from the Hebrew and Greek in some 6,653 places. There are thousands more, but I stopped counting. Which is the most accurate English translation and the closest to the Hebrew and Greek? The answer is the King James Bible.

Certainty Disdained by Some

> **#56 Issue:** Dan Wallace said, "we've replaced the pursuit of truth with the pursuit of certainty." (Script, p. 9)

> **Comment by Dr. Waite:** God **does** want us to be certain. In Proverbs 22:20-21 the Word of God says,
>
> > Proverbs 22:20-21 *"Have not I written to thee excellent things in counsels and knowledge, 21 That I might make thee know the **certainty of the words of truth**; that thou mightest answer the words of truth to them that send unto thee?"*
>
> God wants us to have certainty concerning His Words. It appears that Dan Wallace does NOT have CERTAINTY concerning the very Words of God.

> **#57 Issue:** Dan Wallace said: "they don't have the same manuscripts in front of them, so they don't have certainty. Only Protestants have had to wrestle with this problem." (Script, p. 9)

> **Comment by Dr. Waite:** Those who had the Traditional Text (the Textus Receptus) in their hands **did** have the same manuscripts. Dan Wallace is trying to say that the divergence between the Textus Receptus manuscripts is so great that they are different. You cannot say that. There may be slight spelling variations or other small differences, but for all intents and purposes they did have the same manuscripts. Have Dan Wallace and his other friends exactly collated all 5,255 manuscripts that we have available? No, they haven't. All they can come up with is a wild guess of six to ten differences per chapter (and if this guess is anywhere near being correct, [and I am not admitting this] the differences would be mainly spelling differences. How can Dan Wallace arrive at such a total? Where is his

research? Even Westcott and Hort themselves said that these Textus Receptus type of manuscripts were basically the same. They called them "one voice."

Doctrines Are Involved in the "Variants"

#58 Issue: Dan Wallace quoted a Roman Catholic who said: "Look at all these variants." (Script, p. 9)

Comment by Dr. Waite: This variant emphasis is unfounded! The texts and the manuscripts that underlie the King James Bible are NOT that variable. Instead, they are remarkably identical in all MAJOR areas! It was because these more than 99% of the Greek manuscripts that have been preserved for us were so unified that Westcott and Hort had to make up an unproven reason to combat such unity. They did this in order to convince the world that the less than 1% of the available Greek manuscripts (including their precious B and ℵ) represented the true New Testament text. If you want to speak about variants then we would have to look at the false text that Dan Wallace favors, and the NIV favors, and the NASV favors, and all the other new versions favor. The 5,604 variants between the B/ℵ text and the Textus Receptus average 15.9 variants **per page**. These are different Greek words, not merely spellings, but **words. This is per page, not per chapter. Now, that's real variation!!**

#59 Issue: Dan Wallace said: "Strong, evangelical, conservative Christians began to look at the variants and they said, 'We don't find any doctrines affected by these variants. So what's the problem here?'" (Script, p. 9)

Comment by Dr. Waite: Dan Wallace is now looking at the variants between the Textus Receptus and the Westcott and Hort type of text. This is completely different from saying that the manuscripts that the Christians were using had so many wide-spread differences within themselves.

Dan Wallace's statement that no "**doctrines**" are affected by these variants is absolutely wrong as we have pointed out before. Dr. Jack Moorman listed a total of 356 doctrinal passages where the Westcott and Hort text differs from the Textus Receptus. I have listed 158 of those doctrinal passages in our Chapter V of my book, *Defending the King James Bible*. You can read in detail about the doctrines that are affected by these new versions. Some of the theological categories where doctrinal errors are found in Greek texts and English translations are:

Theology Proper (the doctrine of God)
Ecclesiology (the doctrine of the church)
Angelology (the doctrine of angels)
Satanology (the doctrine of Satan)
Bibliology (the doctrine of the Bible)
Eschatology (the doctrine of last things or prophecy)
Soteriology (the doctrine of salvation), and

Christology (the doctrine of Christ).

For the details on any of these doctrinal errors in the Westcott and Hort texts and/or the NIV, NASV, NKJV footnotes, and the New Berkeley, you can consult Chapter V of the above book, pages 131-183 (5th printing).

What About the Septuagint (LXX)?

#60 Issue: Arthur Farstad said that God "used the Septuagint . . ."

Comment by Dr. Waite: He takes the position, as most of the teachers who teach in the various Christian colleges and seminaries that the Septuagint was B.C. (Before Christ). Though certain PORTIONS of the Old Testament were undoubtedly available in Greek B.C., I believe that the Septuagint Greek translation of the entire Old Testament was A.D. (in the year of our Lord, Anno Domini) rather than B.C.. We would differ on this point. According to the *International Standard Bible Encyclopedia (I.S.B.E.)*, the Septuagint is an extremely inferior translation from Hebrew to Greek for the most part. In some places it is more accurate than others. I don't know how much God "used the Septuagint." He has committed Himself to honor His Hebrew Old Testament, certainly not any sloppy paraphrase of that Divinely inspired, inerrant, infallible Bible such as the LXX.

The Geneva Bible

#61 Issue: Samuel Gipp had a book that said the "founding fathers" of our country quoted from the King James Bible, not the Geneva Bible. (Script, p. 10)

Comment by Dr. Waite: This may be true, but the first settlers were said to have brought the Geneva Bible with them. If the Bible was taken from the texts that underlie our King James Bible, that's fine. Those early Bibles **were** taken from those proper texts. The Geneva Bible was based on the Traditional Text/Textus Receptus as was the Great Bible, the Bishop's Bible, and the Coverdale Bible. These were not taken from the Westcott and Hort type of New Testament text as the New American Standard Version, the New International Version, the New King James in the footnotes. and the other modern versions.

Letters for the NIV Side

#62 Issue: Kenneth Barker said his files were full of letters from people saying they were blessed by using the NIV. (Script, p. 10)

Comment by Dr. Waite: This may be true that there has been a blessing, but the New International Version is not running on full 8 cylinders (if it is an 8 cylinder car). It is running on about 4 cylinders or less. I say this because of its dropping out of 2,886 Greek words from its text. I say this also because of its use of dynamic equivalency of adding to God's Words, subtracting from God's Words, and changing of God's Words. People who do not know the difference do not know all of what God has said.

In What Sense Does the KJB "Preserve"?

> **#63 Issue:** Kenneth Barker said: "Sam [Gipp] quoted the *King James* about the words of the *King James* being preserved." He was referring to Psalm 12:6-7. (Script, p. 10)

Comment by Dr. Waite I don't agree that Psalm 12:6-7 refers to the English words of the King James Bible being preserved. That verse refers to the Preservation of God's Hebrew Old Testament Words, and, by analogy, God's Greek New Testament Words. There was no such language as English at the time this Psalm was written.

There is a secondary sense in which the King James Bible preserves in English those Hebrew and Greek Words which God has Preserved for us. This is possible because the King James Bible accurately translates every Hebrew and Greek Word into the English language so the English speaking world can understand the Preserved Hebrew and Greek Words.

The NIV's Serious Errors in Psalm 12:6-7

> **#64 Issue:** Kenneth Barker said of Psalm 12:6-7 that the "them" refers to people. (Script, p. 11)

Comment by Dr. Waite: Let's examine what the New International Version has done to Psalm 12:6-7. They have made two errors from the Hebrew. They have not translated accurately. Here is Dr. Kenneth Barker trying to argue for his translation saying that 95% of Hebrew Scholars would agree. What the NIV is doing is **interpreting** Psalm 12:1-5 rather than **translating**. There is quite a difference between the two. Dr. Barker interprets verse 7 as a reference to people and therefore puts in the pronoun "us."

The New International Version says for Psalm 12:6-7:

> *"(6) And the **words** of the LORD are **flawless**, like silver refined in a furnace of clay, purified seven times. (7) O LORD, you will keep **us** safe and protect **us** from such people forever."*

These two words "us" are not in any Hebrew text, and he knows it! Kenneth Barker should tell the people listening to this telecast that "us" is not found even one time, let alone two times in Psalm 12:7. This is a serious mistranslation. It is a serious error. The NIV has also omitted a second use of "**words**" from verse 6. The word, "flawless," completely leaves out the Hebrew word for "**words**."

The King James Bible reads for Psalm 12:6-7:

> *"(6) The **words** of the LORD [are] pure **words**: [as] silver tried in a furnace of earth, purified seven times. (7) Thou shalt keep **them**, O LORD, thou shalt preserve **them** from this generation for ever."*

The clear reference to "**them**" is to the "**words**" of the Lord that He has promised to "**keep**" and "**preserve**."

The Hebrew reads for psalm 12:6-7 (which is changed to verses 7-8):

‪(6) 7 אִמֲרוֹת יְהוָה אֲמָרוֹת טְהֹרוֹת כֶּסֶף צָרוּף בַּעֲלִיל‬
‪לָאָרֶץ מְזֻקָּק שִׁבְעָתָיִם׃‬

In verse 6 (or Hebrew verse 7), the two enlarged Hebrew words (*amarOth*) are both properly translated in the King James Bible as "**words.**" This emphasizes the fact that God is talking about keeping and preserving His **WORDS**. By eliminating one of the "**words,**" the NIV makes another error in translation.

‪(7) 8 אַתָּה־יְהוָה תִּשְׁמְרֵם תִּצְּרֶנּוּ מִן־הַדּוֹר זוּ לְעוֹלָם׃‬

In Hebrew grammar, pronouns that are direct objects of verbs are attached to the end of those verbs as suffixes. Notice that I have enlarged two Hebrew verbs, both of which end with a direct object pronoun as a suffix. In verse 7 (or Hebrew verse 8) the Hebrew suffix on the verb "keep" is "them" (*tishmerEm*). It is NOT "**us**" as the NIV wrongly has. It is "**them.**" The Hebrew suffix on the verb "preserve" is literally "him" (*titsrenU*). The King James Bible properly uses "them" in both places to keep the sense parallel. The New King James and the American Standard Version of 1901 both translate these pronouns in this way as follows:.

"You shall keep them, O LORD, You shall preserve them from this generation forever." (NKJV)

"Thou wilt keep them, O Jehovah, Thou wilt preserve them from this generation for ever." (ASV of 1901)

  Dr. Jack Moorman has written an excellent article on this very verse. It is about 10 pages. If you would like to receive it, write us or call us and we will tell you how to get it. Kenneth Barker's NIV is not a translation. It is paraphrase or adding, subtracting, and changing the Words of God. If the NIV rendering were given in a first year Hebrew class as a translation of the Hebrew text, such a recitation would receive an "F" grade.

Preservation of "Jot's" and "Tittles"

#65 Issue: John Ankerberg stated: "Even **if** we're talking about the words being protected, ..." He didn't accept the fact of Bible preservation. He put it in an "IF" clause. (Script, p. 11)

  Comment by Dr. Waite: The Words **have** been protected by the Lord. This is called Bible preservation. Bible preservation is a fact. It was promised by the Lord, and it has been fulfilled by the Lord. It is not a theory or something that has been dreamed up. This is what John Ankerberg is trying to knock out of the context.

  In Psalm 105:8, God said, *"He hath remembered His covenant forever. The Word which He commanded to a thousand generations."* Do you know how many years a generation is? Well, if it is 20 years in a generation, a thousand generations would be 20,000 years. If it is 30 years in a generation, it would be 30,000 years. That is a long time!

In Proverbs 22:20-21, God said:

*"Have not I written to thee excellent things in counsels of knowledge that I might make thee know **the certainty** of the Words of truth, that thou mightest answer the Words of truth to them that send unto thee."*

John Ankerberg is not clear with his question. It sounds like he is not sure about the promise of Bible preservation.

In Matthew 5:17-18 the Lord Jesus said:

*"Verily I say unto you, Till Heaven and earth pass one **jot** or one **tittle** shall in no wise pass from the law, till all be fulfilled."*

The smallest Hebrew letter is the jot, or the yodh.

יִרְאוּנִי is a Hebrew word that begins and ends with this "jot" or "yodh." You can seen that it resembles our comma or single quotation mark. There is no Hebrew consonant smaller than the "jot" or the "yodh." Psalm 119:77

וְאֶחְיֶה is a Hebrew word that has (from left to right, for our English readers), both a "he" and a "cheth." The first letter from the left is a "he." The third letter from the left is a "cheth." Do they not appear similar? The only difference between these two Hebrew letters is the presence or absence of a gap or a space in the upper left portion of the letters. This is a "tittle." It is the smallest distinguishing feature between two Hebrew letters.

בְּכָל is a Hebrew word that has both a "caph" and a "beth." The second letter from the left is a "caph." The third letter form the left is a "beth." Do they not appear similar? The difference between the two letters is that one is curved and the other straight. Also, the "beth" has a slight extension on the bottom right of the letter. This distinguishing feature is called a "tittle." It is the smallest distinguishing feature between two Hebrew letters. This is Bible preservation, is it not? There are many other verses which speak of Bible preservation. We must believe in it and proclaim it!

Inspiration & Preservation--Connected

#66 Issue: Dan Wallace said: "This is one of the amazing fallacies of the *King James* Only school. It assumes that inspiration has a direct corollary in preservation." (Script, p. 11)

Comment by Dr. Waite: If you believe that inspiration (God breathing out the inerrant words of Hebrew and Greek) is NOT correlated with God's preservation of those words; something is wrong with your thinking process. If you don't have a Bible that has the Hebrew and Greek preserved, then what value is inspiration? I believe that God not only gave us verbal inspiration (the words), plenary inspiration (the full inspiration of all of the 66 books of the Old and New Testament), but also He gave us inerrant and infallible preservation. Westcott and Hort did not believe that even the originals were infallible. They state so in their introduction of the Greek New Testament. We believe (in the Bible for Today and the Dean Burgon Society) that God has given to us His Words, breathed out, from Himself in the Hebrew and Greek text verbal, plenary, inerrant, and infallible. We also believe that since God was so careful to give us God-breathed (inspired) verbal, plenary, inerrant, and infallible words that He has also preserved every single word. He promised to preserve His Words, and He has kept that promise.

Textus Receptus--99% of the Manuscripts

#67 Issue: Dan Wallace said: "He [God] has inspired one text, which text has He preserved?" (Script, p. 11)

Comment by Dr. Waite: As far as I'm concerned He has preserved the New Testament Textus Receptus which underlies the King James Bible. As of 1967, by count of the apostate German textual critic from Munster, Germany, Kurt Aland, we had a total of 5,255 manuscripts that have been preserved for us today. Though a few more were added since that time, this includes the following: Papyrus=81; Uncials=267; Cursives=2764; Lectionaries=2143. Dr. Jack Moorman, in his excellent book, *Forever Settled*, made some classifications of these manuscripts. Listed below are the approximate numbers of both the Westcott and Hort kind of manuscripts as well as the Textus Receptus kind of manuscripts which underlie our King James Bible:

	Westcott & Hort MSS	Textus Rec. MSS	Totals	% of MSS WH/TR
Papyrus Fragments:	13	75	81	15%/85%
Uncials:	9	258	267	3%/97%
Cursives:	23	2741	2764	1%/99%
Lectionaries:	0	2143	2143	0%/100%
Totals:	*45*	*5210*	*5255*	>1%/<99%
	>1%	<99%	100%	

Notice that this is only a total of **45** Westcott and Hort manuscripts out of a total of 5,255. In the Textus Receptus tradition there are **5,210 manuscripts.** That's **less than 1%** for the Westcott and Hort text and **more than 99%** for the Textus Receptus text that underlies our King James Bible. Which text do you think that God has preserved? Do you think it is the text that has **less than 1%** of the evidence or **more than 99%** of the evidence? I believe that God has preserved His Words in the Textus Receptus that underlies our King James Bible. Many of the men who are teaching in the Bible schools, colleges, universities and seminaries believe that the Words of God are preserved in approximately 45 manuscripts. In so doing, they discard the other 5,210 manuscripts. In my opinion, this is both illogical and unreasonable.

Erasmus Attacked Again

#68 Issue: In stating what he called the fallacy of the *King James* Only school, Dan Wallace said: "That means that either the Roman Catholic Erasmus changed the text and he was somehow under inspiration, or the King James translators were somehow under inspiration." (Script, p. 11)

Comment by Dr. Waite: This statement has no basis whatever. Why is this charge even made? To this point, no one on this program has said that either Erasmus or the King James translators were "under inspiration." Inspiration means to breathe out ("*All scripture is given by inspiration of God* [breathed out by God]") These **men** were not "breathed out" or "inspired." The "Roman Catholic Erasmus" was not "breathed out" or "inspired." Erasmus had the right Greek text. He was the greatest Greek scholar on the European continent of his day, but he was not "breathed out" or "inspired." The King James translators were not "inspired" either. Men are not "inspired," only the Old Testament and New Testament Words of the Hebrew and Greek were "inspired" or "breathed out" by God. The only man on the panel who erroneously stated that men were "inspired" was James White. This is found on page 26 above as "**#35 Issue.**" It is taken from page 6 of the script.

#69 Issue: Dr. Chambers could only say a few words (Script, p. 11).

Comment by Dr. Waite: Dr. Chambers, who stands for the King James Bible, has only one inch of space on the Script at this point. There is no fairness in this exchange of ideas. It is extremely unbalanced from the amount of time the speakers have to express their point of view--especially if they stand for the King James Bible.

#70 Issue: Dan Wallace said, "But the preserved text, we're talking about a *Textus Receptus* where Erasmus had to invent a lot of readings on the basis of the Latin . . . [in] the last six verses of Revelation . . . he created 17 variants that are not found in any Greek manuscripts." (Script, p. 11)

Comment by Dr. Waite: I do not believe that Erasmus created 17 variants that are not found "in any Greek manuscript." I do not believe he created them "on the basis of the Latin." If you compare the last six verses of Revelation in the Revised Standard Version (based on the Nestle-Aland Greek text) with the King James Bible (based on the Textus Receptus Greek text) you will find they are basically the same. One of the differences is "the **tree** of life" (RSV) versus "the **book** of life" (KJB). I believe the correct rendering is "the **book** of life" as the King James Bible translates it. Dr. Jack Moorman has a book which gives us the documentation as to why it should be "The Book of Life." The book is *Early Manuscripts and the Authorized Version*. It is **B.F.T. #1825**, pages 153-154.

III.
COMMENTS ON PROGRAM #3
Script, Pages 12-17

The KJB Is Not Just Another "Version"

> **#71 Issue:** John Ankerberg referred to the *"NIV Bible,"* the *"New American Standard Bible,"* but the *"King James VERSION."* (Script, p. 12)

    Comment by Dr. Waite: John Ankerberg called the NIV a Bible and the NASV a Bible, but the KJB a version. I call the King James Bible the Bible. I've examined every word of the New American Standard Version and I've found over 4,000 examples of adding, subtracting, or changing the Words of God as found in the Hebrew and the Greek. I've examined every word of the New International Version and have found over 6,653 examples of adding, subtracting, or changing the Words of God as found in the Hebrew and the Greek. In my opinion, these are only "VERSIONS." They are NOT "BIBLES" since they do not translate properly and accurately all of the Hebrew and Greek words found in the Bible!

Version Editors and the Occult

> **#72 Issue:** John Ankerberg said that the King James Bible defenders claim the editors of the NASV, NIV, and NKJV have "an occultic bent." (Script, p. 12)

    Comment by Dr. Waite: Dr. Chambers has never said that there is "an occultic bent" to these editors. This is John Ankerberg's way of pulling in an argument out of nothing. He has falsely charged ALL of the King James Bible defenders thereby. He did not even define his term, "occultic bent." Certainly Bishop Westcott, who was one of the "editors" of the English Revised Version of 1881, had an "occultic bent." Is John Ankerberg denying Westcott was a member of the occult "Ghostly Guild"? The evidence is clear in *Life and Letters of B. F. Westcott* which is available as **B.F.T. #1866**, 928 pages, for a GIFT of **$45 + P&H**. The proof of his connection with the "Ghostlie Guild" is found in Volume I, page 117 of this book.

NIV/NASV/NKJV Men vs. Erasmus' Skill

> **#73 Issue:** John Ankerberg praises the qualifications of "Dr. Gleason Archer." (Script, p. 12)

Comment by Dr. Waite: If Dr. Gleason Archer is so highly qualified in this area, and such an expert, why wasn't he on this program? John Ankerberg told me originally that Dr. Archer was going to be one of the participants.

> **#74 Issue:** John Ankerberg said to the KJB men: "Are you saying that Gleason Archer and Art and Ken and Don over here, with all of their degrees and all their information can't do as good a job as the guys like Erasmus?" (Script, p. 12)

Comment by Dr. Waite: Here John Ankerberg is boasting about the degrees of all of these men. They are trying to come up to Erasmus' knowledge. Erasmus was the greatest Greek scholar on the European Continent in his day. These fellows apparently think that they know all there is to know. I do not think they could do as good a job in the area of the Greek language as Erasmus did. First of all the analogy is wrong. Erasmus did not **translate** the New Testament. He assembled a Greek text and had it printed. Secondly, Erasmus was no ignoramus. To think that the knowledge of Greek and Latin of our 1900's can measure up to that of the 1500's when Erasmus was living is ridiculous. There is no comparison between the two scholastic and educational climates.

The NKJV vs. the King James Bible

> **#75 Issue:** John Ankerberg said of the representative of the *New King James*, "If you really want the *Textus Receptus*, he's got it!" (Script, p. 12)

Comment by Dr. Waite: The New King James Version claims to use the Textus Receptus, but I stumbled across at least 2 or 3 places where they used the Westcott and Hort critical text. I have not made a thorough check. There may be hundreds of other places involved! In the footnotes of the study addition of the New King James Version the editors either praise or use the Majority text of Hodges and Arthur Farstad. They also either praise or use the NU text (Nestles/ United Bible Societies text) which is the modern counterpart of the Westcott and Hort critical text.

> **#76 Issue:** Arthur Farstad mentioned various words in the King James Bible that were no longer used. (Script, p. 13)

Comment by Dr. Waite: Lawrence Vance has written a book called *The Archaic Words in the King James Bible*. This book is available from the BIBLE FOR TODAY. It is **#B.F.T. #2719**, 591 pages, @ **$20.00 +P&H**. He quotes periodicals and books showing where and how these so-called "archaic" words of the King James Bible are in current use. It becomes obvious that many of the KJB's so-called "archaic" words are still in use in modern times.

James White Again

#77 Issue: After Samuel Gipp spoke, James White spoke of Mrs. Gail Riplinger's position. (Script, pp. 13-14)

Comment by Dr. Waite: James White was trying to say that Samuel Gipp is going to take Gail Riplinger's position. She wasn't on the broadcast. She can take her own position. She is quite good at defending herself. She doesn't need Dr. Gipp or anyone else to do so in absentia.

#78 Issue: James White made extraneous remarks. (Script, p. 14)

Comment by Dr. Waite: James White doesn't contribute anything that is germane to the argument that is being discussed at this time.

#79 Issue: James White talked about Revelation 14:1. (Script, p.14)

Comment by Dr. Waite: James White took one verse to prove that the Textus Receptus is in error. How does James White know that the Textus Receptus is in error in Revelation 14:1? This is only his opinion. Where is his proof positive? He does not bring if forth, he just says it without proof or documentation.

Samuel Gipp, KJB, and "Inspiration"

#80 Issue: Don Wilkins said to Samuel Gipp: "Well, so the *Textus Receptus* isn't important, it's just the *King James*." (Script, p. 15)

Comment by Dr. Waite: Here Don Wilkins is getting Sam Gipp into a corner saying that the Textus Receptus is not important. The Hebrew and Greek texts that underlie our King James Bible are the basic starting points of the King James Bible. If we throw away the starting points, then we have nothing. The King James Bible in English is the most accurate English translation of the Bible, but we must also defend the Hebrew and Greek texts which underlie this Bible. Again, let me say that God's promise to preserve His Words of the Bible involves His Hebrew and Greek words. It does not involve the words in English, Spanish, French, German, or any other language.

#81 Issue: In a series of interchanges with Don Wilkins, Samuel Gipp implied or stated that the King James Bible was "inspired." (Script, p. 13)

Comment by Dr. Waite: If Samuel Gipp is going to say that one English Bible is "inspired" then how about all of the other English Versions? The King James Bible is a **translation**. I believe it is the most accurate translation that we have. It can be properly called "the Word of God kept intact in English." I can't say that about the NIV, the NASV, or the NKJV. But the King James Bible was

NOT "breathed out by God" or "given by inspiration of God." It was a translation by men. This distinction must be clearly drawn. If a person believes that the King James Bible is "inspired" or "God-breathed" just like the Hebrew and Greek originals, after God has closed the canon, then how can we be sure that modern Versions or even the Book of Mormon are not also inspired? The men who are in the charismatic movement believe the "revelations" that they speak are also "inspired." This is not the case. God closed the canon after the book of Revelation. These men are using this to hammer away at the King James Bible. I do not agree with Samuel Gipp on this point.

More of James White

> **#82 Issue:** James White quoted Dr. Strouse that "Christians en masse have always believed this traditional text . . ." (Script, p. 15)

Comment by Dr. Waite: Here James White is quoting Dr. Strouse, but Dr. Strouse can't get very many words of his own even though he is one of the participants on the program. Dr. Strouse believes as I do that the words of preservation have to do with the Hebrew and Greek words and not the English words.

> **#83 Issue:** James White mentioned Luke 22 and Revelation 16:5 and condemned the King James Bible's wording. (Script, p. 16)

Comment by Dr. Waite: Before this debate ever took place, John Ankerberg assured me that if there were specific verses that were going to be discussed the men would know ahead of time. I told John Ankerberg that James White would bring up specific verses without prior knowledge not the others, and, true to form, he did. I object to this unfairness!

James White Quotes *Defending the KJB*

> **#84 Issue:** James White gave a partial quote from my book, *Defending the King James Bible.* He quoted the phrase: "the diabolical nature of the New King James Version. . ." (Script, p. 16)

Comment by Dr. Waite: This is right. I do believe that the New King James is diabolical. James White was quoting from *Defending the King James Bible*, but he did not quote even the entire sentence. In fact, the partial quote does not even make up a sentence. The New King James in its footnotes quotes the Nestle/Aland text, the United Bible Societies text (NU), and The Majority text (M.T.). This leaves the reader wondering which is right. The NKJV also uses over 2,000 dynamic equivalencies which either add to God's Words, subtract from God's Words, or change God's Words in some other way. This is exactly what Satan did in the Garden of Eden. In my considered opinion, it is a "diabolical" methodology, no matter who makes use of it!

#85 Issue: James White quotes from this writer, "D. A. Waite."
(Script, p. 16)

Comment by Dr. Waite: James White tried to get involved with what I've said and written.

#86 Issue: More on James White's quoting of me. (Script, pp. 16-17)

Comment by Dr. Waite: What I was saying in the words that James White quoted was that there is a diabolical methodology used by he New King James Version in that they, like Satan, add to, subtract from, or change God's Words. As far at their use of footnotes, if they don't know what the Words of God are they should say so rather than giving all possibilities. This is most confusing both to new Christians as well as to mature Christians.

IV.
COMMENTS ON PROGRAM #4
Script, Pages 17-24

Mrs. Riplinger's Book Unjustly Attacked

#87 Issue: Don Wilkins said of Mrs. Riplinger's *New Age Bible Versions*, "virtually everything she says is either a misquotation or a misleading of the truth." (Script, p. 17)

Comment by Dr. Waite: This is not true. Mrs. Gail Riplinger has documented all 700 pages of her book, *New Age Bible Versions*. Has Don Wilkins checked out ALL 1500 footnotes in her book? If so, how many of the 1500 does he accuse her of "misquoting" or of being "misleading"? Though there is room for disagreement in some things, as always in any book ever published, I believe there is a tremendous value in her book. It is a book that has sold over 100,000 copies. It has been used to awaken many people as to Bible version perversion.

Westcott & Hort--"Fine Christian Men"?

#88 Issue: Don Wilkins said: "She (Mrs. Riplinger) focuses on among other things Westcott and Hort. And these were <u>fine men</u> of the church, <u>fine Christian men</u>." (Script, pp. 17-18)

Comment by Dr. Waite: In the back of her book Mrs. Riplinger has taken the time to go through for us *The Life and Letters of Westcott*. This biography was written by Westcott's son, Arthur. Also she has gone through *The Life and Letter's of Hort* written by Hort's son, also named Arthur. These were mostly letters written by Westcott and Hort to each other, or to other people. In this comment Don Wilkins says that Westcott and Hort were "**fine Christian men**." This is false! What is meant by "**Christian**"? They were theological heretics and apostates! I would not term such "**fine Christian men**." Let me tell you what these "**fine Christian men**" believed about the inerrancy even of the originals. This quote is from their *Introduction to the Greek New Testament* on page 280,

> *"Little is gained by speculating as to the precise point at which*
> *such **corruptions** came in* [he is talking about corruptions of the

Greek text] ***they may be due to the original writer*** [In other
words Paul may have made an error at the very start of his
original text. Can you say that this is a "**fine Christian man**"
who said there were errors in the original writings?] *or to his
amanuensis if he wrote from dictation, or they may be due to one
of the earliest transcribers.*"

The Westcott and Hort position is that the "errors" in the Greek text, as they
consider them to be errors and corruption, may be due to the "**original writers**. "
This would mean that there was never at any time inerrancy in the Scriptures, even
in the very originals themselves. We have written an entire booklet called *The
Theological Heresies of Westcott and Hort* (**B.F.T. #595 @ $3+P&H**). In this
booklet, I have taken about 125 of their quotations from their own writings. Here
is an example written by Westcott to Hort from volume I, page 207 of *The Life and
Letters of B. F. Westcott* on May 5, 1860:

> *"My dear Hort--. . . for I too `must disclaim setting forth
> infallibility' in the front of my convictions. . . . At present I find
> the presumption in favor of the absolute truth--**I reject the word
> infallibility**--of Holy Scripture overwhelmingly."* [Arthur
> Westcott, *The Life and Letters of B.F. Westcott*, Vol. I, p. 52]

Mr. Wilkins may believe that Westcott and Hort were very "**fine Christian men**"
who rejected the infallibility of the Scriptures, but I do not. I think they are
apostates and diabolical. They are questioning the very Words of God.

What about Westcott's belief in miracles? This quote is taken from *The Life
and Letter's of Westcott* , volume I, page 52 written by his son. This was taken
from his diary on August 11, 1847:

> *"I never read an account of a **miracle** but I seem instinctively to
> feel **its improbability**, and discover some want of evidence in the
> account of it."*

Don Wilkins says that Westcott and Hort were "**fine Christian men**." I do not
think that they are "**fine Christian men**" if they reject the authenticity of the
miracles of the Lord Jesus Christ.

Here is another example from *The Life and Letters of B. F. Westcott* Volume
II, page 69, written on March 4, 1890, written to the Archbishop of Canterbury:

> *"No one now, I suppose **holds that the first three chapters of
> Genesis, for example, gives a literal history. I could never
> understand how anyone reading them with open eyes could
> think they did.**"*

Here is Bishop Brooke Foss Westcott, a man who Don Wilkins believes was a "**fine
Christian man**," denying the authenticity and historicity of Genesis 1-3 as literal
history. In other words, there was no Adam and Eve. There was no Garden of
Eden. There was no fall of man. There was no creation of the heaven and the earth
by God in six solar days. All of these, according to Westcott, are not "literal

history." Is this a "**fine Christian man**"? NO, this is a liberal apostate.

As far as Westcott's clever denial of the resurrection of the body of the Lord Jesus Christ is concerned, he does not believe in a bodily resurrection. I have written a book on this subject entitled *Bishop Brooke Foss Westcott's Clever Denial of Christ's Bodily Resurrection.* It is **B.F.T. #1131**, 38 pages, @ **$4** **+P&H.**. I analyzed two of Westcott's own books and showed clearly that he did not believe in the bodily resurrection, the bodily ascension, or the bodily return of the Lord Jesus Christ.

On this same subject of the bodily resurrection, let me quote from Kirsopp Lake's book *The Immortality in the Modern Mind* (1922, pages 38-40),

> *"Until the middle of the 19th century* [1850], *the opinion in England maintained the same position as Catholic theologians. They held uncompromisingly to the opinion demanded by the Apostle's Creed, and affirmed the resurrection of the flesh. . . .* ***Bishop Westcott is really the author of the great change. He entirely abandoned belief in the resurrection of the flesh as formulated in the creed***; *but he never said so. On the contrary, he used all his matchless powers of shading language, so that the change from white to black appeared inevitable, natural, indeed scarcely perceptible."*

In *The Historic Faith* from the article "I believe in the resurrection of the flesh," page 136 Westcott commented as follows:

> *"The 'flesh' of which we speak as destined to a resurrection is not that material substance which we can see and handle, measured by properties of sense."*

In other words, there is no resurrection of the real body, the flesh. Then Kirsopp Lake continued:

> *"Thus he explained that when the Creed spoke of the resurrection of the body it did not mean the resurrection of the flesh(though both in the Greek and Latin originals it said so), but it was affirming the survival of personal identity."*

The man whom Don Wilkins' calls a "**fine Christian man**" is denying the resurrection of the flesh of the Lord Jesus Christ.

What about the "fine Christian man," Professor Fenton John Anthony Hort? Hort wrote to Rev. J. B. Lightfoot on May 1, 1860. It is found in *Life and Letter's of F. J. A. Hort* (volume I, page 420). Hort wrote:

> *"If you make a decided conviction of the absolute infallibility of the New Testament sine qua non of cooperation, I fear I could not join you. . . ."*

Hort did not believe in the infallibility of the New Testament. How can he be a "**fine Christian man**."

Then, in a letter written to Rev. John Ellerton on July 9, 1848, (from *Life and*

Letter's of F. J. A. Hort, volume I, page 78) Hort said:

> *"I'm inclined to think that no such state as `**Eden**,' (I mean the popular notion) ever existed, and that **Adam's fall** in no degree differs from the fall of each of his descendants as Coleridge justly argues."*

Do you think this is a "**fine Christian man**," a man who denies the fall of man as recorded in Scripture?

Note what Dr. Hort wrote about Charles Darwin:

> *Have you read **Darwin**? How I should like to talk to you about it! In spite of difficulties, I'm inclined to think it **unanswerable**. In any case it is a treat to read such a book."* [Arthur Hort, *Life and Letter's of F. J. A. Hort*, Vol. I, page 414]

I disagree completely with Don Wilkins in saying that Westcott and Hort were "**fine Christian men**." These men, Westcott and Hort, were both doctrinal apostates.

On May 2, 1860, writing to Westcott, as found in the *Life and Letter's of F.J.A.Hort*, Volume I, page 422, by Hort's son) Hort said,

> *"But I am not able to go as far as you in asserting **the absolute infallibility** of a canonical writing."*

He denies the infallibility of the Lord Jesus Christ's Words.

He wrote in January, 1886, to Mr. H. Brinton. He referred to Article IX of the *39 Articles of the Anglican Church*. Those are the articles that the Anglican Church believes and stands for. Hort said:

> *"The authors of the Article doubtless assumed **the historical character of the fall in Genesis**. This assumption is now, in my belief, **no longer reasonable**. But the **early chapters of Genesis** remain a divinely appointed **parable** or apologue setting forth important practical truths on subjects which, as matters of history, lie outside our present ken."*

What do you assume when you read the book of Genesis? Do you assume that when God wrote about the sin of man in Genesis Chapter 3, that this was an historical account? Do you believe that there was a decree given to man not to eat of the fruit of the tree of the center of the garden? Don Wilkins is berating Mrs. Riplinger for criticizing Westcott and Hort. He then says these men were "**fine Christian men**." These men were heretical apostates and NOT "**fine Christian men**." Is that what you think about the "**early chapters of Genesis**"? These chapters include such things as: the universal flood of Noah, the tower of Babel, the creation by God of all the things in Heaven and in earth, and the creation by God of man rather than by evolution. Dr. Wilkins says they were "**fine Christian men**." It's hard to believe that Don Wilkins would call men who believe the "early chapters of Genesis"are only parables "**fine Christian man**."

We have reproduced *The Life and Letters of Hort* and also *The Life and Letters of Westcott*. If you would like to receive them you may by contacting The

Bible For Today. They are **B.F.T. #1866** and **B.F.T. #1867**. Each is two volumes and over 900 pages in length. They are $48 and $45 +P*H respectively.

Westcott & Hort's Manuscripts "Best"??

#89 Issue: Don Wilkins said of Westcott and Hort's text, "our use of it has become the text that most of us use and we think it's the best manuscripts [sic]." (Script, p. 18)

Comment by Dr. Waite: The New Testament Greek text that evolved from Westcott and Hort is the worst text. This text was a revolutionary change and an attack on the Traditional Greek text that had been received by the churches for 1500 years. In my book, *Defending the King James Bible,* I point out the manuscript authority of our Textus Receptus and the scarcity of manuscripts that go along with Westcott and Hort. They simply have B and ℵ and about 43 other documents. This is less than 1% of the evidence. What is worse, these two manuscripts are extremely unreliable.

Westcott and the "Ghostly Guild"

#90 Issue: Don Wilkins quoted from the Westcott and Hort biographies. (Script, p. 18)

Comment by Dr. Waite: Here again Don Wilkins is quoting from the books *The Life and Letter's of Westcott* and *The Life and Letters of Hort.* Why doesn't Don Wilkins get a copy of this book and read it and see for himself about these quotations. His interpretation of the Ghostly Guild would be corrected. He wouldn't excuse Westcott like he did if he had read those 1800+ pages carefully.

#91 Issue: Don Wilkins said of Westcott's relation with the Ghostly Guild that Mrs. Riplinger's description "was just the opposite of what was true and it's a deliberate misstatement of the facts." (Script, p. 18)

Comment by Dr. Waite: As far as Westcott's association with the Ghostly Guild, he was one of the founders of it. In volume I on page 117 in *The Life and Letters of B. F. Westcott,* Westcott's son, Arthur, wrote of his father,

> "He devoted himself with ardor, during his last year at Cambridge, to two new societies. One of these was **the`Ghostlie Guild.'** . . . The Ghostlie Guild . . . was established for the **investigation of all supernatural appearances and effects.**"

Westcott went into Spiritism and talking to the dead. This was all part of their investigation of "supernatural appearances" and ghosts. That was why it was called the "**Ghostly Guild.**" This is a matter of fact. If Don Wilkins looked at these biographies (*The Life and Letter's of Hort* and *The Life and Letter's of Westcott*) he could read about this Ghostly Guild. If speaking to the dead wasn't spiritualism I don't know what is. He based his unscriptural practice of speaking to the dead spirits on the Apostles Creed. He gets this from twisting the words "The communion of the saints." He believed that after you die you still should have communion of the saints. The book, *The Revelation of the Risen Lord*, was written by Westcott in 1881. This was the same year that Westcott and Hort came out with their false Greek text that underlies these false versions today. On page 10 of this book Westcott wrote:

> ". . . that in Him He may lift our eyes to Heaven our home and find it about us even here. [he believed that Heaven was here] That in Him [Christ] we may be enabled to gain some sure confidence of *fellowship with the departed.*"

He wanted to have fellowship with those who have departed from this life. He was into Ghostly Guildism and Spiritism no matter what Dr. Wilkins calls it.

James White Justifies Westcott's Error

#92 Issue: James White claimed Westcott "frequently spoke of Roman superstitions" as if he was against them, thus trying to sanctify Westcott's theology. (Script, p. 18)

Comment by Dr. Waite: These men, Westcott and Hort, didn't speak of "Roman superstitions" as being against them. They were in favor of the Roman Catholic Church. They were in favor of the "superstitions" of Rome. They attempted to get the whole Anglican Church back to the Roman Catholic system, in fact. They were deeply involved in the Anglo-Catholic movement of their time.

Mrs. Riplinger--Attacked and Defended

#93 Issue: James White, speaking of Mrs. Riplinger, said, "it's easier for people to go ahead and bend the facts, bend the truth to try to promote this conspiracy." (Script, p. 18)

Comment by Dr. Waite: You need to get Gail Riplinger's book and read it. There are 700 pages in it with almost 1500 footnotes bristling with documentation on the New Age quotations indicating what they believe. It also has excellent quotations from the new versions (NIV, NASV and so on). She has a tremendous appendix with chapter and verse showing how Westcott and Hort were heretics religiously as well as in their other beliefs.

#94 Issue: Speaking of the other men's quotes against Mrs. Riplinger, Dr. Chambers said: "none of the rest of us knew they were going to pull out those examples." (Script, p. 18)

Comment by Dr. Waite: When I talked to John Ankerberg and asked him what was going to be on this telecast, he said that the men who participated would know exactly what would be discussed. Any particular Bible verses or quotes discussed would be given ahead of time to all. Here, Dr. Joseph Chambers makes it very clear that John Ankerberg did not tell him in advance that these portions of Gail Riplinger's book would be discussed and she would be condemned.

Had he known in advance, he would have been able to answer the statements.

> **#95 Issue:** Dr. Chambers said of Mrs. Riplinger's book, though she may have made some mistakes, like all of us do, "I do not believe she purposely misquoted." (Script, p. 19)

Comment by Dr. Waite: I agree with Dr. Chambers. Every author, and speaker makes mistakes. She has had five printings of that book so far. She has sold over 100,000 copies of this book. She plans a 6th printing soon. She has many facts in her book and also many opinions. She is entitled to her opinions. I may not share all of her opinions, but I think *New Age Versions* is a valuable and helpful book. She is not the type of person who would purposely misquote. Mrs. Waite and I have met her. Mrs Waite interviewed her on video. This video is available. If you are interested in seeing the lady, and she is a lady, Mrs. Riplinger, you need to get this video. It is **B.F.T. #2545VC1-2 @ $25 +P&H**. If she has made an error of fact or quotation, she is willing to admit it and correct it. Mrs. Riplinger has written four or five other books in her field of interior design as well. She is not a "new author," nor is she unfamiliar with doing documented research.

"Lucifer" Is Not "The Morning Star"!

> **#96 Issue:** Kenneth Barker commented on Isaiah 14:12 and Mrs. Riplinger's discussion of it. He said of the Latin Vulgate's rendering of it: "All they were doing was translating the Hebrew 'morning star' into Latin and it was 'Lucifer.'" (Script, p. 19)

Comment by Dr. Waite: Is this correct? Is the Hebrew really "morning star" or is it not? I would recommend that you order the Bible For Today **#2509 @2/$1.50**. It is a short little paper that I put together entitled "In Defense of Lucifer, Shining One" (from Isaiah 14:12). There is no Hebrew word for "star" in this verse at all. Dr. Kenneth Barker has made another serious error here. He can talk all he wants about being a Hebrew scholar, but this mistake indicates that he is in error and does not really know his Hebrew language and the literal meaning of Hebrew words.

There is no "Morning Star" in the Latin Vulgate either. First of all I took the interlinear Hebrew Bible on page 2 of the paper. I went into what the exact Hebrew word is and what it means. The Hebrew word is *helel*." This word is wrongfully translated as "shining star" in the interlinear. I don't agree with that translation. It is really "**shining one**" or "**Lucifer**" which means "**light bearer**." It comes from two Latin words, *lux* ("light") and *ferre* ("to bear or carry"). That word Lucifer is a good translation for *helel*.

I wanted you see what the Hebrew word was so you could see what I was talking about. Then, I went over to the *Analytical Hebrew and Chaldee Lexicon* by D. Davidson put out by Samuel Baxter and Sons. Then, I turned to page 4 under *helel* which is the masculine, singular noun that's translated "Lucifer" in our

King James Bible and is translated the "morning star" in the NIV and some of these other versions. I find out in the *Analytical Hebrew and Chaldean Lexicon* that *helel* comes from the verb *halal*. On page 5, I went over to *halal* because that is the word that *helel* comes from. What does it mean? It means "**to shine**."

There is no "morning star" here. It is true that stars shine, but the verb doesn't mean "star" or "morning star" it only means "**to shine**." If you look further you will find the noun *helel* (from Isaiah 14:12). The meaning of it you will find is "**shining one**." There is no word for "star" here. Then I looked in the *Hebrew and English Lexicon of the Old Testament* by William Gesenius translated by Edward Robinson, edited by Brown, Driver, and Briggs. On page 8 of the paper, we that the verb, *halal,* means "to shine." It is used in the noun form (*helel*) when it says, "His lamp (*helel*) shone upon my hand." In Isaiah 13:10 we see the translation is to "**flash forth light**." So, it has to do with "**shining and light**." If you look up *helel*, the masculine noun, you see the meaning is, "**the shining one**."

How would "**the shining one**" be translated in Latin? I majored in Classical Greek and Latin in the University of Michigan and in the Latin course that I took (or in any good Latin dictionary) I found simply that "Lucifer" comes from two Latin words (you can look this up in any English dictionary): *lux* or *lucis* which comes from the word for "light." We have Lux soap. Lux is also used in our camcorders to indicate the degrees of "light." We have *fer* which comes from *ferre* or *fero* (in both Greek and Latin). This means "to carry or to bear." So, **Lucifer** means "**the one who bears or carries light**, or **light bearer**." "**Shining one**" is certainly a good translation. Somebody who bears light is certainly shining. There is no problem with using **Lucifer**. Where does Dr. Kenneth Barker and his New International Version get "Morning Star" for this Hebrew word?

In the first place, there is no "morning" here. In the second place, there is no word for "star" here. This is an **interpretation** and not a translation. Dr. Chambers didn't have a chance to mention that one of the Lord's titles in Revelation is "The Bright and Morning Star." Here they have the Satanic Lucifer (remember in Isaiah 14 the five "I Wills") called the "morning star." This is wrong to have Satan have the same title as the Lord Jesus Christ. Remember also that one of the other titles for **Lucifer** or the "**Shining One**" is an "**angel of LIGHT**."

2 Corinthians 11:14 *"And no marvel; for **Satan** himself is transformed into **an angel of light**."*

#97 Issue: Kenneth Barker said: "Why should we bring over into English a term that means 'morning star' in Latin?" (Script, p. 19)

Comment by Dr. Waite: It does NOT mean "morning star" in Latin as we have shown clearly above. It means "**Shining One**" or "**Lucifer.**".

#98 Issue: John Ankerberg, in speaking of "morning star" as used in the NIV, said: "they translate that word accurately." (Script, p. 20)

Comment by Dr. Waite: That is a very false statement. The Hebrew word for "morning" is *boqer*. The Hebrew word, for "star" is *kokav*. If you look in Genesis 1:13 you see the Hebrew word for morning is *boqer*. Look in Genesis 1:16 and see that the Hebrew word for "star" is *kokavim*. This is plural. You can see that the Hebrew word, *helel*, found in Isaiah 14:12 has NOT been translated accurately. It was translated inaccurately in the NIV.

#99 Issue: John Ankerberg, again referring to the Isaiah 14:12 "Lucifer" debate, said: "We don't have to make up anything." (Script, p. 20)

Comment by Dr. Waite: Who is making up anything? The word "**Lucifer**" in the King James Bible comes from the Hebrew word, *helel*. It means "**light bearer**" or "**shining one**." "Lucifer" means "light bearer" or "shining one" and is a proper translation for the Hebrew word. "Morning star" is an improper and false translation of this word. It is an interpretation, rather than a translation.

#100 Issue: John Ankerberg said Mrs. Riplinger had said that the editors of "new translations" had gone insane, died, etc." (Script, p. 20)

Comment by Dr. Waite: John Ankerberg is trying to be folksy. Gail Riplinger does not phrase it this way. He is misconstruing this

#101 Issue: Kenneth Barker said: "You can have a false morning star and a true morning star." (Script, p. 21)

Comment by Dr. Waite: There is no "morning star" of any kind, either false or true. It is "Lucifer." In Isaiah 14:12, you have a "shining one, a light bearer." In 2 Corinthians chapter 11:14 it says that "Satan himself is transformed into an angel of light." This is the "shining one, light bearer," or Lucifer in Isaiah 14:12. He is the fallen angel that has said "I will" to God 5 times (Isaiah 14:13-14). His last "I will" is "I will be like the Most High." He is also mentioned in 2 Corinthians 11:13-15. This is a perfect picture of the way **Lucifer the light-bearer** operates and deceives people by transforming himself into an "angel of LIGHT." The NIV has Satan usurping the title of the Lord Jesus Christ given to Him in Revelation 22:16:.

> Revelation 22:16 *"I Jesus have sent mine angel to testify unto you these things in the churches. I am the root and the offspring of David, [and] the bright and morning star."*

#102 Issue: Dan Wallace said: "I don't think Satan is ever called Lord Jesus Christ, though. That's a proper noun." (Script, p. 21)

Comment by Dr. Waite: This argument about common nouns and proper nouns is false as well. The Lord Jesus Christ, in Revelation 22:16, is called "the bright and morning star." "Morning star" in Revelation is a compound common noun or a noun phrase the same as "morning star" is in Isaiah 14:12 in the NIV. It consists of two common nouns, "morning" and "star." To say as Dan Wallace said that the morning star in Revelation is a proper noun because it is the name of a person is absolutely false. Though it **REFERS** to a proper noun, the Lord Jesus Christ, it is not in and of itself a proper noun. It is a common noun. Here are the English grammatical definitions of common and proper nouns: A "common noun" is the name of a person, place, thing, or idea." A "proper noun" is the name of a particular person, place, thing, or idea." If this is the case then you could say that the Isaiah 14:12 morning star in the NIV is a proper noun referring to Satan, but this is not the case. Both are common nouns.

Bagster's *Analytical Greek Lexicon*

#103 Issue: Dan Wallace said: *"Analytical Greek Lexicon.* This was done over a hundred years ago by Samuel Bagster." (Script, p. 22)

Comment by Dr. Waite: So what! Is he saying that languages change in 100 years? Both classical and New Testament Koine Greek are "dead language." They do not change. We don't want to update the Bible into modern Greek. There is nothing wrong with Samuel Bagster's *Analytical Greek Lexicon.*

#104 Issue: Samuel Gipp said: "I bought an *Analytical Greek Lexicon.* I got it when I was in Bible college 20 years ago, not a hundred years ago." (Script, p. 22)

Comment by Dr. Waite: This is true, Samuel Bagster's *Analytical Greek Lexicon* is still published by the Hendrickson Publishers. It has been revised slightly by Perschbacher and is now called the *New Analytical Greek Lexicon.* It now contains both the Textus Receptus words and the Westcott and Hort words used in their respective Greek New Testaments. This makes it useful for comparative purposes.

Can English "Correct" Hebrew & Greek?

#105 Issue: Samuel Gipp said: "I don't think you can enlighten anything on the King James Bible by going to the Hebrew/Greek." (Script, p. 22)

Comment by Dr. Waite: This is the Peter Ruckman position which I disagree with. Just as I warned John Ankerberg when he wanted me to appear on the program, Dr. Gipp served as a lightening rod to take the attention off of the main subject. Was that the main subject--to make all King James Bible advocates appear like the Samuel Gipp/Ruckman position in order to tarnish the entire cause? The King James Bible is a translation from the Hebrew and Greek. The source of The King James Bible is **not** the King James Bible itself!

The source of the King James Bible was the Hebrew and Greek text that had been providentially Preserved by God through copies of the original manuscripts. The men who translated our King James Bible into English translated it from these Hebrew and Greek copies. We believe that the King James Bible is the Word of God in English. It is God's Word kept intact in English. It is profitable to study the Hebrew and Greek text underlying the King James Bible to find the various treasures and word pictures there. Peter Ruckman says that the King James Bible corrects the Hebrew and Greek text and contains what he calls "advanced revelation." We in the Bible for Today and the Dean Burgon Society do not agree with this position.

Samuel Gipp makes yet another error. Those of us who stand for the King James Bible as the most accurate English translation, believe it for four reasons: (1) It has superior texts of Hebrew and Greek. (2) It has superior translators. (3) It has superior technique of translating, and (4) It has superior theology. We do **not** say that we can **not** go back to the original languages of Hebrew or Greek to expound on the text.

Greek Lexicons and English Dictionaries

#106 Issue: James White talked about Samuel Gipp's Greek lexicon: "When it contradicts the King James translation, what do you do?" (Script, p. 23)

Comment by Dr. Waite: James White is trying to say that lexicons in the Greek language contradict the King James translation. I do not believe that any lexicons contradict the King James translations if they are sound and complete lexicons. One modern Hebrew lexicon is the *Gesenius Hebrew Lexicon*. A modern Greek lexicon was edited by Rudolf Kittel's son, Gerhard Kittel. It has many of the New Testament Greek words. I have those 10 volumes. Gerhard Kittel was a friend of the Nazis. He wanted to exterminate the Jews. Mrs. Gail Riplinger has documented some facts about this man in her book, *New Age Bible Versions*. She has extensive documentation in her book. You may have the Gerhard Kittel lexicon, or other lexicons that go along with the New International Version, but the lexicons that are sound and sensible do not contradict the King James Bible.

#107 Issue: Dan Wallace asked Samuel Gipp, "Do you use an English dictionary?" (Script, p. 23)

Comment by Dr. Waite: The men are all needling Samuel Gipp. This is what I told John Ankerberg. In so doing, they missed the important serious textual questions. They strove "about words to no profit" (2 Timothy 2:14). I do not believe, as I've said before on the broadcast, that the King James Bible has any, what I call, "translation mistakes."

There are two parts to this issue: #1 You can find at least one of the meanings given in the Hebrew or Greek language that the King James writers have selected for their translation. One of the meanings that was current in 1611 in the English language was selected by the King James translators. #2 They followed at least one of the rules of Hebrew and Greek syntax and grammar in their translation. So, they have at least one of the meanings of the Hebrew or Greek words (there may be other meanings) and used at least one of the syntactical or grammatical rules of Hebrew or Greek There may be other syntactical rules that may have been used, but they used at least one, and been faithful. Therefore, I don't believe that there are any "translation mistakes" in the King James Bible.

I don't think that you can produce a sound Greek lexicon that does not at least contain one of the words that the King James translators have used from the Hebrew and the Greek.   These men were linguistic giants as far as their qualifications. There is not a single person on this panel who can equal the King James Bible translators and their linguistic capabilities. We have gone into this in great detail in our book, *Defending the King James Bible*. If you are interested in this book call us at, 1-800-John 10:9 and we'll tell you how to obtain your copy. This book has 5 main chapters in it. Chapter I talks about the Biblical preservation of God's Words in Hebrew and Greek. Chapter II talks about the superior texts of Hebrew and Greek. Chapter III talks about the superior translators. If you want to know about the King James Bible translators' linguistic and translation qualifications you can look in Chapter 3.   Chapter IV takes up the superior technique of translation. Chapter V discusses the superior theology.

#108 Issue: Dan Wallace asked Samuel Gipp: "would you encourage the lay person who reads the King James Bible to use an English dictionary"? (Script, p. 23)

Comment by Dr. Waite: You would be all right if you use a dictionary that has valid English meaning, like the *Oxford English Dictionary*--either the 2 volume microprint, or the 14-16 volume set. This gives the historical meaning of every English word. Every word that is in the King James Bible is in the *Oxford English Dictionary* along with the meaning current in 1611.

#109 Issue: Dan Wallace asked Samuel Gipp again about his understanding of the King James Bible without a dictionary. (Script, p. 23)

Comment by Dr. Waite: This question was beside the point. This was supposed to be a high-level discussion about the different versions and here these men are jumping on Samuel Gipp, for a solid page and a half in the Script, for Samuel Gipp's strange statements. He doesn't seem to know what he is talking about on this issue. If I had been asked what dictionary I used as far as the King James Bible is concerned, I would have recommended *The Oxford English Dictionary*. It has the historical meanings from the English words from 1000 A.D., 1200 A.D., 1500 A.D., 1611 A.D., 1700 A.D., 1900 A.D. and so on. This is what I use.   When someone accuses the King James Bible translators of making a translation mistake, I look up the word in the *Oxford English Dictionary* to see what the word meant in 1611 and I find the translation to be accurate.

Changing Meanings--KJB vs. Others

#110 Issue: Dan Wallace discussed the number of words that have

changed their meanings since 1611. (Script, p. 23)

Comment by Dr. Waite: As far as the number of words that have changed their meaning in the last 386 years is concerned; the *Word List* of the Trinitarian Bible Society lists about 600 words and the American Bible Society's dictionary of New Words lists about 500 words. Samuel Gipp said there were only "30" that have changed. I am sorry that Samuel Gipp didn't know the number of words that have changed their meanings. It is unfortunate that he is there without these details. I would have been glad to have been there if there had been any opportunity to have a logical, high level discussion about the Greek and Hebrew text, the superiority of the King James Bible, the errors of the New International Version, the errors in the New American Standard Version, and the errors in the New King James Version. I am unhappy that these five men are putting all their argument against the King James Bible and permitting the multiple errors of the other versions to go unchallenged. This is wrong and unbalanced. This is what I predicted to John Ankerberg that would happen, and it did happen.

#111 Issue: There was more discussion on words that had changed their meanings. (Script, p. 24)

Comment by Dr. Waite: There is an entirely new book that has just come off the press. It is called, *Archaic Words and the King James Bible*. There are over 700 words that the author deals with. The author shows how many of these "archaic" words are still used today. He searched libraries, books, magazines, newspaper, and all other places and found that many of these words are still being used. The point of the book is to show that these words are not so archaic after all. In the appendix of this book the author compares some of the new versions and how they use these same "archaic" words that the King James Bible uses.

#112 Issue: James White continued attacking Samuel Gipp on word meanings. (Script, p. 24)

Comment by Dr. Waite: This is why we need a dictionary to tell the meaning of these words in 1611. As mentioned before, I recommend that you buy the *Oxford English Dictionary*.

#113 Issue: Speaking of the King James Bible compared with the modern ones, Dan Wallace said: "yours is changing far more than ours is." (Script, p. 24)

Comment by Dr. Waite: The King James Bible is not changing more than any translation. You have five men on the program who are **against** the King James Bible and **for** these other perversions. I have analyzed these three major versions that are represented by these men and I have found the following data:

- **The New King James Version has over 2,000 dynamic equivalency changes.**
- **The New American Standard Version has over 4,000 dynamic equivalency changes.**
- **The New International Version has over 6,653 dynamic equivalency changes.**

These changes include adding to God's words, subtracting from God's Words, and changing of God's Words in some other manner. The meaning of about 500 English words may have changed slightly in the King James Bible, but that is an infinitesimal amount compared with the almost 800,000 words in the King James Bible. The King James Bible translators did not use dynamic equivalency. They translated with a verbal equivalence technique with the English meaning of 1611.

V.
COMMENTS ON PROGRAM #5
Script, Pages 24-31

"Child" vs. "Servant" and "Son"

#114 Issue: Samuel Gipp pointed out that in four places the new versions change "child Jesus" to "servant Jesus." (Script, p. 25)

Comment by Dr. Waite: The word is *paidion* which comes from *pais* and sometimes *pais* is used. *Pais* occurs 24 times in the King James Bible. In 13 of the 24 times, it is translated other than "servant." *Paidion* occurs 5 times and is NEVER translated "servant" in the King James Bible. The very word, "pediatrician" in English comes from this "ped" root. It refers to "CHILD" or "CHILDREN." He is a children's doctor. He is not a "servant's doctor."

#115 Issue: Samuel Gipp said Acts 4:27 and 4:30 should have been "<u>child</u> Jesus." (Script, p. 25)

Comment by Dr. Waite: That's right. They should have left in the word, "child." They had no authority to take it out.

#116 Issue: Samuel Gipp said that "When it talks about a lost nobleman's son, they don't have any problem making *pais* a son . . ." (Script, p. 25)

Comment by Dr. Waite: This is a good point. *Pais* or *paidos* is the word for "child" or "son." We have the very word in the English language. Pedagogy comes from *paidos*, meaning "child" and *agO*, meaning "to lead." It means a leading of a child along the path to understanding and learning. The word, "pediatrician" is another word that has the Greek word for "child" in it. It comes from *paidos* ("child") and *iatros* ("physician"). It is a doctor for children. We don't call a "pediatrician" a doctor of <u>servants</u>. We don't call a "pedagogue" someone who "teaches servants."

#117 Issue: Arthur Farstad said to Samuel Gipp: "I know you don't believe in the Greek, but the Greek says *pais*. It does not say *huios* which is the word for 'son.'" (Script, p. 25)

     Comment by Dr. Waite: No, this is not true. Though some contexts translate it "servant," *pais* does not mean servant in its original, primary meaning. *Pais* means "child." It is a male child, it is "son." If it is a female child, it is "maid" or "maiden."

Joseph vs. "Child's Father"

#118 Issue: In discussing Luke 2:33, the KJB has "Joseph and his mother." The NIV has a false text and reads "The child's father and mother." Kenneth Barker doesn't answer this clear difference. (Script, p. 26)

     Comment by Dr. Waite: Why not give the Textus Receptus the credit it ought to have in Luke 2:33. It clearly says "Joseph and His mother." Why make a change in this to read, "His father and His mother"? This NIV reading could deny the virgin birth.

#119 Issue: John Ankerberg asked Kenneth Barker about his NIV, "Did you take out all the verses about the virgin birth?" (Script, p. 26)

     Comment by Dr. Waite: Nobody has said that all the verses about the virgin birth have been taken out of the New International Version. This is a false point, but Kenneth Barker did not answer this directly.

The Deity of Christ--NIV vs. KJB

#120 Issue: Kenneth Barker referred to D. A. Carson's chart in his book, *The King James Version Debate*, where he claims that the NIV has "more clear, explicit references to the Deity of Christ than the *King James Version* does." Samuel Gipp didn't agree. (Script, p. 27)

     Comment by Dr. Waite: I don't agree either. If you look at that chart as I have looked at it, the chart **implies** that the New International Version has more references to the Deity of Christ than the King James Bible does. If you examine the references you see that this is simply not true. The King James Bible refers equally as much, if not more, to the Deity of Christ in the verses that are selected by D.A. Carson. This is a false chart and a false charge. A complete analysis of D. A. Carson's erroneous book is available as **B.F.T. #99-101**. This item is three 2-hour cassette radio tapes, @ **$9.00 + P&H**.

The 1 John 5:7-8 Battle

#121 Issue: When John Ankerberg began the discussion of 1 John 5:7, he said, "Sam [Gipp], what's the objection, first of all?" (Script, p. 27)

     Comment by Dr. Waite: Why does he continually pick on Dr. Gipp? Why didn't he turn to Dr. Joseph Chambers? Why didn't he turn to Dr. Thomas Strouse? Why did he turn only to Dr. Samuel Gipp? He's not the only one on this team that stands for the King James Bible.

> **#122 Issue:** Samuel Gipp said, "Well, the verse has been removed. There is no 1 John 5:7." He's talking about the NIV now. (Script, p. 27)

Comment by Dr. Waite: Actually, this portion that is left out is a part of verse 7 and a part of verse 8. It is not I John 5:7 in its entirety. It is the last part of verse 7 that is left out and the first part of verse 8. That is a misleading statement of the problem that is frequently made. I would have expected better of Samuel Gipp, however.

What Does "Perfect" Really Mean?

> **#123 Issue:** Samuel Gipp said: "I believe the *King James Bible* is perfect." (Script, p. 27)

Comment by Dr. Waite: Why did Samuel Gipp use the word "perfect" when referring to a translation? I believe that God is perfect. I believe that the Lord Jesus Christ is perfect. I believe that man is imperfect, and anything he does or produces is also imperfect compared with God's absolute perfection. I realize that God wants us to be perfect for He is perfect. I realize that we cannot attain to that, but some people take that word to mean no blemishes whatsoever. The King James translators were men, just men. They were depraved men as all men are. That is a misleading statement to say that the King James Bible is "perfect" if you mean 100% "perfect" and is "inerrant," without any errors of any kind, even spelling or typographical--in other words, as "perfect" as God is. This is a term which I personally use either for the Hebrew and Greek originals or for the Hebrew and Greek accurate copies that underlie the KJB.

I believe that the King James Bible is the most accurate translation in the English language that is in existence. Which King James Bible did Samuel Gipp mean which was "perfect"? Is it the Cambridge edition or the Oxford edition? I stand for the King James Bible without any apology, but let me tell you that the Cambridge edition of the King James Bible is more accurate than the Oxford edition. Let me quote to you from the *Dean Burgon News* the December, 1990, issue on page 3, where I wrote,

> *"It has been pointed out to us that there are various variations in the King James Bibles produced in England or the United States of America. Those produced by the Cambridge University Press follow more accurately the original A.V. 1611 in certain places, while those printed by the Oxford University Press depart in these places. Most of the publishers in this country follow the Oxford wording, though some have a mixture. I'll give three examples. The first is in Jeremiah 34:16, in the middle of this verse the Cambridge, the A.V. 1611, and the Hebrew have, 'Whom ye had set at liberty'. While the Oxford*

> *and most U.S. King James Bibles have 'Whom **he** had set at liberty'"*

Now my friend, let me be honest with you. In Jeremiah 34:16 the Oxford University Press King James Version edition is wrong, false, and in error. The Cambridge is on target, it should be **ye**. Am I supposed to say that the King James Bible is perfect? Are you talking about the Cambridge edition or the Oxford edition? It **is** the most accurate in the English language, but I would not use the word "perfect."

> *"Let's look at another example. In 2 Chronicles 33:19 in the first part of this verse the Cambridge edition, the A.V. 1611, and the Hebrew have, 'and all his **sin**.' The Oxford Bible, and most King James Bibles in the U.S. have, "And all his **sins**."'*

My friend, that is an error in the Oxford editions.

> *"The third example is in Nahum 3:16. At the end of this verse the Cambridge, A.V. 1611, and the Hebrew Bible all say, 'And **flieth** away.' Where the Oxford edition and most Bibles in the United States have, 'And **fleeth** away'. "Flieth" is the correct translation. Though these variations are slight and few in number they do point out the human weaknesses and frailties that are found in printing presses and their books, even in the King James Bible. Why not check these three verses in your Bible to see if you have a Cambridge edition, Oxford edition, or a mixture of the two?"*

1 John 5:7-8 Defended

#124 Issue: Samuel Gipp defended old evidence favoring 1 John 5:7-8, including Tatian's *Diatessaron*. (Script, p. 27)

Comment by Dr. Waite: Dr. Samuel Gipp has said this correctly. 1 John 5:7-8 is in Tatian's *Diatessaron*. If you want the very finest and the briefest summary of the evidence I would suggest you get the analysis of 1 John 5:7-8 by Dr. Jack Moorman. You will find this in Chapter 6 in his book, *When the KJV Departs From the so Called Majority Text*. This is **B.F.T. #1617**, 160 large pages, @ **$16.00 + P&H**. Dr. Moorman gives the evidence of modern textual criticism and how it undermines 1 John 5:7-8. Modern textual critics say that there are **only four** Greek manuscripts that back these verses.

Dr. Moorman documents the evidence in favor of 1 John 5:7-8, both the internal evidence as well as the external evidence. Under the external evidence he lists, not 4 Greek manuscripts, but 9 different manuscripts that have 1 John 5:7-8, this disputed passage on the Trinity. These manuscripts are: (1) 61, (2) 88 mg., (3) 221 mg., (4) 429 mg., (5) 629, (6) 635 mg., (7) 636 mg., (8) 918, and (9) 2318.

Other Eastern witnesses containing 1 John 5:7-8 include: (1) some Syriac Peshitto manuscripts; (2) the Syriac Edition at Hamburg; (3) the Bishop Uscan Armenian Bible; (4) the Armenian edition of John Zohrob; (5) the first printed

Georgian Bible; and (6) a few recent Slavonic manuscripts.

Early Latin witnesses containing 1 John 5:7-8 include: (1) Tertullian (died 220 A.D.; (2) Cyprian of Carthage (died 258 A.D.); (3) Priscillian (358 A.D.); (4) The Speculum (5th century A.D.); (5) A Creed called the Espositio Fidei;(5th or 6th century A.D.); (6) Old Latin (5th or 6th century A.D.); (7) A Confession of Faith of Eugenius, Bishop of Carthage (484 A.D.); (8) two works of Vigilius of Thapsus, North Africa (490 A.D.); (9) Fulgentius of Ruspe in North Africa (died 533 A.D.; (10) the prologue to the General Epistles of the Latin Vulgate; (11) Cassiodoris of Italy (480-570 A.D.). It is also in hundreds of Latin manuscripts.

Don't say "Throw out the King James Bible," because you can see that it is correct. How did these people get this passage if it was not there in the original? We believe that it was taken out by an Arian (one who did not believe in the Trinity) who was the head of the Greek Orthodox Church. He removed all the manuscripts that dealt with the Trinity. Frederick Nolan discusses this possibility at length in his excellent book, *Inquiry into the Integrity of the Greek Vulgate*. This is **B.F.T. #1304**, 604 pages, @ **$30.00 + P&H**.

#125 Issue: **Dan Wallace gave the line that Erasmus had someone make up a manuscript that had in it 1 John 5:7-8. (Script, p. 27)**

Comment by Dr. Waite: This is false. This is the old lie that many have been telling for years, but it is still not true.

#126 Issue: **Speaking about 1 John 5:7-8, Dan Wallace said: "We have six, at most, late manuscripts." (Script, p. 27)**

Comment by Dr. Waite: Well, maybe they're late, but there are not only 6 manuscripts there are 9 manuscripts, as listed above in **#124 Issue**. Don't forget either that there are **hundreds** of Latin manuscripts that are not mentioned here yet do contain 1 John 5:7-8.

#127 Issue: **Regarding 1 John 5:7-8, Dan Wallace said: "As far as we know, it's not in any manuscript until the sixteenth" [century]. (Script, p. 27)**

Comment by Dr. Waite: Let's look at these manuscripts: #61 (16th century), #88 (in the margin, 12th century), #221 (in the margin, 10th century), #429 (in the margin, 14th century), #629 (14th century), #635 (in the margin, 11th century), #636 (in the margin, 15th century), #918 (16th century), #2318 (18th century). There are **only 3 manuscripts from the 16th century or later**. 6 of these are earlier. Here Dr. Wallace says that he does not know any manuscripts that are before the 16th century. Dr. Wallace's statement is incorrect.

#128 Issue: **Dr. Strouse said: ". . . Gaussen a century ago, Dabney a century ago said there's a grammatical problem if you . . ." (Script, p. 28)**

Comment by Dr. Waite: Dr. Strouse is interrupted and not allowed to finish his sentence. I think that this is unfair that he is not allowed to speak. He was the best qualified man on the King James Bible side to have explained the internal evidence clearly. Yet he was precluded from doing so. If Dr. Strouse would have spoken he would have pointed out the following truth. If you take out the center part, of 1 John 5:7-8 you would have an error in Greek grammar or syntax. Leaving 1 John 5:7-8 intact, this error in Greek grammar or syntax would disappear. Dr. Strouse did not get a chance to explain this internal evidence for the passage.

Bible Editors Losing Their Voices

#129 Issue: John Ankerberg attacked the *New Age Bible Versions* that spoke of some Bible correctors losing their voices. (Script, p. 28)

Comment by Dr. Waite: Do you remember earlier in the transcript that some of the translators of these new Bibles, after making their corrections of the text lost their voices in some way. John Ankerberg turned to one of these men to comment on this, and **that man immediately lost his voice and was unable to speak**. During the time when talking with John Ankerberg about my appearing on the program, I asked him if he ever edited our remarks. This was important to me if I were to have been on the program. He assured me that he never edits anything in the middle of a program. Sometimes he takes things from the end of the program if it is too long. In this case, however, John Ankerberg edited out that entire context of his this participant losing his voice. This is significant I think. Kenneth Taylor, the editor of the Living Version told *Time Magazine* that he had lost his voice after working on that version. He himself attributed it to his tampering with God's Words. When John Ankerberg saw that one of the men had lost his voice, he stopped the tape, and cut it out of the telecast. Two men who were on that program told me these details, Dr. Joseph Chambers and Dr. Thomas Strouse. By the mouth of two witnesses it was factually true and it happened, even though it has been denied by some.

130 Issue: John Ankerberg said Mrs. Riplinger's book said: "that the editors of the *NASB, NIV* and *New King James*, as a result of their working and thinking, five have lost their voices, one has gone insane and another died prematurely." (Script, p. 28)

Comment by Dr. Waite: He's misquoting Gail Riplinger. You will not find Mrs Riplinger saying that about the editors of the New American Standard Version, the New International Version, or the New King James Version. She was talking about all different types of versions and editors who have changed the Textus Receptus, going back many scores of years. She included people in the days of Westcott and Hort, for instance. This is not a true statement on John Ankerberg's part. He should get the exact page, and quote her exactly if he can find this statement in her book!

> **#131 Issue:** In talking about this same theme, John Ankerberg said of Mrs. Riplinger: "she says it's the new versions, the translators's of the new versions." (Script, p. 28)

Comment by Dr. Waite: Gail Riplinger clearly means from the context of her remarks, "new versions" other than the King James Bible. This goes back to the English Revised Version of 1881, the American Standard Version of 1901, the *Phillips Version*, the Living Version, and all the other versions other than the King James Bible. They are twisting Mrs. Riplinger's words and meanings. This is inexcusable! Was not the English Revised Version of 1881 a "NEW VERSION" compared with that of 1611?

> **#132 Issue:** Dr. Chambers said: "Of course you can go to Phillips, J. P. Phillips. His story is incredible of what happened to him." (Script, p. 28)

Comment by Dr. Waite: John Ankerberg didn't let Dr. Chambers finish his statement about Phillips. He interrupted him in the middle of solid documentation he was about to give.. He didn't interrupt anyone else. This is not fair.

> **#133 Issue:** Though not in the Script as such, this is about where the losing of the voice came up. (Script, p. 29)

Comment by Dr. Waite: Right here is where one of these men was going to comment about Bible editors loosing their voice and the man who was about to answer this question couldn't talk. He lost his voice temporarily. I think it was Dr. Don Wilkins of the NASV. This was taken right out of the telecast and the transcript as well. So much for the truthfulness of John Ankerberg when he told me that he would not "edit out" any remarks during the telecasts (unless they were running overtime, which was not the case here!)

Did the K. J. Translators Know Greek?

> **#134 Issue:** Dan Wallace stated: "the King James translators knew Greek less well than they knew Latin and so they constantly relied on the Latin to get themselves through the Greek." (Script, p. 29)

Comment by Dr. Waite: This is so patently false that I will not let that go uncorrected. In Chapter III of my book, *Defending The King James Bible*, I quote from, *Translators Revived* (page 86) by Alexander McClure about Dr. Lancelot Andrews. This is **B.F.T. #1419**, 260 pages, @ **$13.00 + P&H**. McClure says that "his manual for private devotions prepared by himself is wholly in the Geek language." Do you know of any translator of the New International Version, or the New American Standard Version, or the New King James Version that has a manual of private devotions even in English, let alone in Greek? Does this convince you that Dr. Andrews "knew Greek less well than . . . Latin"? Let me ask you this, do you know of any editor or translator of either the New International Version, the New American Standard Version, or the New King James Version who has prepared for private devotions a manual wholly in the Greek language? The statement made by this gentleman in this transcript, Dr. Dan Wallace, who is on the faculty of Dallas Theological Seminary, is absolutely false.

Take Sir Henry Savile who was in company four of the Oxford group. He translated the six books of the gospels, Acts, and Revelation. Let me tell you some of the background of Henry Savile. He was a tutor in Greek and Mathematics to Queen Elizabeth. That certainly says he knew something about Greek. In Alexander McClure's book *The Translators Revived*, from pages 164-169 it is stated:

> *"Henry Savile published from the manuscripts the writings of 'Bradwardin Against Palagius,' 'the Writers of English History Subsequent to Bede,' 'The Prelections on the Elements of __Euclid__.'"*

Now, Euclid in Geometry was all in Greek. How could he publish these manuscripts and writings if he didn't know Greek? McClure continued:

> *"He is chiefly known, however, for being the first to edit the complete work of Chrysostom, the most famous of the __Greek__ Fathers."*

Notice, "__Greek__" Fathers, not Latin Fathers. John Chrysostom had many pages that he wrote to the people to whom he ministered and Savile was the first to completely edit his work. His edition of 1,000 copies was made in 1613, and makes eight immense folios. A folio is the size of a large dictionary or encyclopedia. That was a monumental task. I don't know any of the modern translators of the new versions (or perversions) who come anywhere near the superiority and skill of this man or other King James translators in their superiority in Greek and Hebrew! See McClure's book for further proof of the falsity of Dan Wallace's statement. It is **B.F.T. #1419**, 260 pages, @ $13.00 + P&H.

Titus 2:13 and the Deity of Christ

> **#135 Issue:** Dan Wallace misquoted what the King James Bible said in Titus 2:13. He said: "they translated it something like this: 'the appearing of the glory of our great God and __OF__ our Savior Jesus Christ,'" as if they are two distinct persons. (Script, p. 29)

Comment by Dr. Waite: Dr. Wallace should have quoted the King James Bible exactly rather than guessing at what it says. The King James Bible in Titus 2:13 says, "Looking for that blessed hope and the glorious appearing of the great God and our Savior Jesus Christ." What's wrong with this? The word, "and" is used in the sense of "even" here, thus identifying the Lord Jesus Christ as both God and Saviour. Dan Wallace has added words and called them the King James. He has misquoted an "opponent" which is a serious error in the battle for truth!

> **#136 Issue:** Dan Wallace, alluding to Granville Sharp, said "the

King James translation here is wrong because it suggests that there are two Persons in view, and there is one in view, the Lord Jesus." (Script, p. 30)

Comment by Dr. Waite: The argument here of Titus 2:13 is not that the King James Bible is in error, regardless of what Dan Wallace has said. The King James Bible **does not** deny the Deity of Christ in this passage. "Looking for that blessed hope and the glorious appearing of the great God and our Savior Jesus Christ." This verse is saying God **even** our Savior. The word in the Greek language is *kai.*" *Kai* means, not only, "and" or "in addition to," but also, "even" which identifies the previous noun as being the same person with another title. The same is the case in English. You can say, "the great God and our Savior." He is called God and Savior both. Just like I am my name and also father, grandfather, and husband. When I call myself "father and grandfather and husband," does that mean that I am three people? No, I am a father and a grandfather and a husband. I'm a grandfather because I have eight grandchildren. I'm a father because I have five children. I'm a husband because I have had one wife for the past 49 years (It will be 50 on August 27, 1998). Dan Wallace is trying to put up a smoke screen in his argumentation. He is attacking the King James Bible without letting Dr. Chambers or Dr. Strouse have a chance to give a rebuttal to his false argument.

At this point, James White talked about the chart in his book. Mr. White got it from D.A. Carson's book. James White should have given D.A. Carson credit for this chart, but he did not. He took all the credit for himself. He said that he "created" the chart, yet it came straight from Carson's book. The verse that should be discussed at this time should be I Timothy 3:16:

> *"Great is the mystery of godliness:* **_God_** *was manifest in the flesh, justified in the Spirit, seen of angels, preached unto the Gentiles, believed on in the world, received up into glory."*

This refers to the Lord Jesus Christ as God and absolute Deity. What do the New American Standard and the New International Versions say? They take the word "**God**" away and substitute "**He**" in its place. These versions do not say anything about God in this verse. This is an important verse that should have been brought out on this program, but Dr. Chambers and Dr. Strouse were not invited to give their side on this issue. Again, fairness has disappeared.

More on 1 John 5:7

#137 Issue: James White said that 1 John 5:7 "is not found in any Greek manuscript in the first 1600 years of the Christian church." (Script, p. 30)

Comment by Dr. Waite: James White is talking about the "first 1600 years"? This is up to the end of the 16th century and the beginning of the 17th century. This is absolutely false. We went over this earlier in this study. [See **#127 Issue** above] 1 John 5:7 is in at least nine manuscripts. Let's look at the dates of these manuscripts: #61 (16th century), #88 (in the margin, 12th century), #221 (in the margin, 10th century), #429 (in the margin, 14th century), #629 (14th century), #635 (in the margin, 11th century), #636 (in the margin, 15th century), #918 (16th century), #2318 (18th century). There is **only 1 manuscript after the 17th century or later**. 8 of the 9 are before the 17th century.

Attack on the King James Translators

#138 Issue: Don Wilkins said: "the reason the King James people didn't get it right was because they were relying on the Latin and Latin doesn't have the word 'the.'" (Script, p. 30)

Comment by Dr. Waite: The Latin doesn't have the word "the"? Does he mean that "the" doesn't exist in the Latin language or does he mean "the" isn't here in this passage in the Latin? This is a little bit strange. Don Wilkins makes the same false assumption that the King James Translators were relying on Latin instead of Greek. Don Wilkins and Dan Wallace should know the difference between *kai* (which means "and" or "even") and something else. Titus 2:13 doesn't say "the great God and our Savior" in the sense of "the great God" and another person, "our Savior Jesus Christ." Apparently these two men do not understand the meaning of the word *kai* or else they wish to falsely accuse the King James Bible's wording as being in error.

The NIV and "Hell"

#139 Issue: Kenneth Barker said: "if you'll take the *NIV* Exhaustive Concordance and look up the word hell you will discover several references to hell in it . . ."(Script, p. 30)

Comment by Dr. Waite: In the King James Bible, here are 54 references to "hell." There are only 14 references to Hell in the NIV and they're all in the New Testament. There's not a single reference to Hell in the Old Testament. In the New Testament, the word, Gehenna is the word that is translated Hell. The NIV doesn't translate "Hades" as "Hell." The Hebrew word for this is "Sheol." In the NIV Old Testament Sheol is not translated "Hell."

Doctrines Are Lost in Versions' Verses

#140 Issue: Dan Wallace said: "If a doctrine has to be found in each verse, then we've lost a doctrine. But if the doctrine is in the Bible and in several other verses, we've lost nothing." (Script, p. 31)

Comment by Dr. Waite: What he is saying here is that we don't need to find the doctrines in each and every verse where they should be located. I am saying if the doctrine is there in the original languages in certain verses, then we should find that same doctrine in these same verses in every English translation. We are not to say, "well, the doctrines are somewhere in the New International Version, somewhere in the New American Standard Version." My friend, if the doctrine is in the King James Bible from the Textus Receptus Greek text which underlies it, then it ought to be in the same verse and the same words in these other versions and perversions. The problem is that sometimes it is not! It is serious error for Dan Wallace to say, "we have lost nothing."

VI.
COMMENTS ON PROGRAM #6
Script, Pages 31-36

Version Accuracy Unanswered

#141 Issue: John Ankerberg opened this Program #6 by asking which of the various versions is the most accurate. (Script, p. 31)

Comment by Dr. Waite: Notice, John Ankerberg doesn't say we are going to defend the New International Version. Nobody on the program to this point has defended the NIV until now. Nobody has defended the New American Standard Version or even the New King James Version. All five men (including John Ankerberg, the host) have been **against** the King James Bible. All they are doing is attacking the King James Bible. They do not give the men representing the King James Bible opportunity to defend the King James Bible or to attack these versions and perversions and give illustrations of their faults. The whole telecast is monopolized by those who are antagonistic towards our King James Bible. I am opposed to this as being grossly unfair to the truth.

John 1:18--False Greek Text in Versions

#142 Issue: In response to the charge that the new versions "watered down" the Deity of Christ, James White said about John 1:18: "what we have here is one of the plain places in the New Testament where Jesus Christ is described by the Greek term *Theos* which means God." (Script, p. 31)

Comment by Dr. Waite: That statement by James White is false. The true and proper reading in the Greek text is as it is in the King James Bible and its underlying Textus Receptus. The Greek is *monogenEs huios*. The proper translation is "only begotten SON." It is not *theos* (God) at all, it is the only begotten "Son." Mr. White's critical Greek text should be rendered "only begotten GOD." This is a Gnostic heresy referring to the Lord Jesus Christ as a created being! This points out the presence of serious heretical doctrine in the false

Westcott and Hort Greek text!

> **#143 Issue:** James White claims "only begotten GOD" is found in the earliest manuscripts of John in John 1:18. (Script, p. 31)

Comment by Dr. Waite: I'd like first of all to get the actual documentation and evidence for "only begotten SON" rather than "only begotten GOD" as the NASV has. The Greek word *theos* does not occur in that place of John 1:18. I'd like to quote from an excellent book written by Dr. Jack Moorman, *Early Manuscripts and the Authorized Version--a Closer Look--With Manuscript Digest and Summaries).* It is **B.F.T. #1825**, 157 large pages, @ **$15.00 + P&H**. On page 100, the Greek documentation is given in favor of the false reading of "the only begotten GOD": P (papyrus) 66, P75, ℵ* (the Sinai Manuscript), ℵ-1, B (which is the Vatican), C*, and L. The different versions are: pc, Peshitto, Harclean-mg, Coptic:ba, and an Ethiopic-rom. That is all there is.

What is the documentation in the Greek for the true reading of "the only begotten SON"? Here are some of the manuscripts: A, C-3, E, F, G, H, K, M, S, U, V, W-supplement, X, Gamma, Delta, Theta, Lambda, Pi, and 063. Here is the Cursive evidence: It's in the so-called MAJORITY text and Family #1 and 13.

Here is the version evidence: the Old Latin manuscripts a, c, e, f, ff2, l, and q. the Latin Vulgate. The Syriac editions: Harklian, Palestinian. The Armenian. The Ethiopic-ppl. It is also extant in: Y, Omega, 047, 055, 0141, 0211, 0233?. Here is what Dr. Moorman concludes in the footnote to that documentation:

> *"This is the classic Gnostic perversion, with its doctrine of intermediary gods. It is the trade mark of corruption in the early Egyptian manuscripts which unfortunately spread to some others."*

This exactly correct! James White either doesn't know what he is talking about, or else he is purposely deceiving his audience. Either alternative is unfortunate.

> **#144 Issue:** Kenneth Barker stated that *monogenEs* meant "one and only" or "one of a kind" or "unique" or "special." (Script, p. 31)

Comment by Dr. Waite: Such is not the case at all. *Mono* means "only." *GenEs* is from the word, *gennaO* which means "to be begotten" or "to beget." The full word, *monogenEs* means "only begotten" exactly as the King James Bible has translated it.

> **#145 Issue:** Kenneth Barker used Hebrews 11:17 as proof of his meaning for *monogenEs* since Isaac is called "only begotten." (Script, p. 31)

Comment by Dr. Waite: I believe that the sense in which Isaac was the "only begotten" son of Abraham was that Isaac was the primary and most important son. He was Sarah's miracle son of her old age. He was a picture of the Lord Jesus Christ. Christ was the "seed" of Abraham. He was the one that would carry the line of the Lord Jesus Christ from Abraham's day down to the day that the Lord Jesus Christ would be born. For all of these reasons, it was fitting for God to call Isaac the "only begotten" of Abraham. This is Biblical typology.

Dean Burgon's Massive Evidence

#146 Issue: Dan Wallace said: "Burgon argued that these early manuscripts were produced by heretics. Without a shred of evidence he argued this." (Script, p. 32)

           Comment by Dr. Waite: Dean Burgon never argued anything "without a shred of evidence"! He had evidence that was bulging at the seams. We have made available five of Dean John William Burgon's books on the evidence that he presents on the Greek text of the New Testament. The five books that we have reprinted are: *Revision Revised* (640 pages, hardback, **B.F.T. #611 @ $25 +P&H**); *The Last Twelve Verses of Mark* (400 pages, perfect bound, **B.F.T. #1139 @ $15 +P&H**), *The Traditional Text* (350 pages copy machine bound, but soon to be hardback, **B.F.T. #1160 @ $15 + P&H**), *Causes of Corruption* (340 pages copy machine bound, but soon to be hardback, **B.F.T. #1159 @ $15 + P&H**), and *Inspiration and Interpretation* (590 pages copy machine bound, but soon to be hardback, **B.F.T. #1220 @ $25 +P&H**). This quote is from *Causes of Corruption of the Gospels* (chapter 13, page 192). Dean Burgon wrote:

> *"It is even notorious that in the earliest age of all, the New Testament Scriptures were subjected to such influences. In the age which immediately succeeded the Apostolic there were heretical teachers not a few, who finding their tenets refuted by the plain Word of GOD bent themselves against the written Word with all their power. From seeking to evacuate its teaching it was but a single step to seeking to falsify its testimony."*

Dan Wallace has made the statement that,

> *"Burgon argued that these early manuscripts were produced by heretics without a shred of evidence."*

Dan Wallace is making statements that he should not make. In Burgon's book, *Causes of Corruption*, (pages 192-202) he talks about Gnosticism and the heretics of that persuasion.

           First of all Burgon mentions the Ebionites. What did they do? *"They interpolated and otherwise perverted one of the four gospels until it suited their own purposes. They used a strangely mutilated and depraved text of Matthew's gospel."*   Marcion flourished about 150 A.D. Burgon said of him: *"He was a heresiarch* [a lead heretic] *who shamefully maimed and mutilated the inspired text. He wrote Marcion's gospel which was known to be a heretical production. It was, in fact, one of the many creations of the Gnostic age. It was a lacerated text of St. Luke's gospel."* Is Dan Wallace right?   Is this not evidence of corruption.

           Burgon wrote: *"Tatian constructed his Diatessaron in which he attempted to weave the four fold narratives of the gospels into one."*

Basilides flourished about 134 A.D. In *The Causes of Corruption* (page 195 and 199) Burgon wrote, "*He and his followers invented a gospel of their own, a gospel of Basilides.*"

Valentinus flourished from about 140 A.D. Burgon wrote: "*He and his followers interpolated and otherwise perverted one of the four gospels until it suited their own purposes.*" This gospel that they perverted was the gospel of John. In fact he wrote a Gospel of Valentinus. Is this "without a shred of evidence"? No! Dean Burgon was loaded with evidence.

On pages 199 and 201 Burgon points out another heretic. He wrote: "*Cerinthus and his heretical followers adopted St. Luke's Gospel and also used an exhibition of Mark.*" Did they not corrupt Luke and Mark? This is a matter of history. How can Dan Wallace speak as he did without any facts at his disposal and say that "*Burgon argued that these early manuscripts were produced by heretics without a shred of evidence.*" Dan Wallace is the man that does not have a shred of evidence, not Dean Burgon! Anybody who has read Dean Burgon knows that Dean Burgon has mountains of evidence.

On page 199, Dean Burgon wrote, "*Heracleon was deliberately censured by Origin for having corrupted the text of the fourth gospel in many places.*" Even Origin, the heretic, said that Heracleon, the heretic, must be censured for having corrupted the text of John.

Burgon wrote about the heretic Theodotus who lived about 192 A.D. (page 204), "*He was a Gnostic who used a depraved copy of John chapter 1 verse 3.*"

Dean Burgon wrote on pages 208,209, "*The Manichaean Heretics used a perverted text of John 10:14-15.*" Is this "without a shred of evidence" that these heretics had a hand in changing the text?

Another heretic that Dean Burgon mentions is on page 207. Manes lived about 261 A.D. and wrote his own fabricated heretical gospel. Dan Wallace should read carefully every page of Dean Burgon's over 2,000 pages in the five books we have made available for all to read. I feel certain that all five of them are in his Dallas Seminary Library. Dr. Wallace has borne major "false witness" against Dean John William Burgon here! (Exodus 20:16)

Heretical Corruption of Manuscripts

#147 Issue: Dan Wallace said: "I don't see any evidence for heretics having produced these manuscripts." (Script, p. 32)

Comment by Dr. Waite: Dan Wallace is misquoting Burgon. Burgon did **NOT** say that heretics **"produced"** manuscripts. He said that heretics **doctored and corrupted manuscripts** produced by others. Burgon's point was that heretics changed manuscripts, not produced manuscripts. As far as Dan Wallace's quotation of Scrivener is concerned, Scrivener is quoted by Dean Burgon in another area. Let me quote Dean Burgon's quotation of Dr. Frederick Scrivener who was on the English revision committee of the English Revised Version of

1881. I might add that he fought against both Westcott and Hort because they were making such strange changes in the Traditional Text. This quote is from Dean Burgon's book, *Revision Revised.* On page 30 Burgon wrote:

> *"'It is no less true to fact then paradoxical in sound,' writes the most learned of the Revisionist body* [notice he is quoting Dr. Frederick Scrivener], *'that the worst corruptions, to which the New Testament has ever been subjected, originated within a hundred years after it was composed: that Irenaeus* [A.D. 150] *and the African fathers, and the whole Western, with a portion of the Syrian Church, used far inferior manuscripts to these employed by Stunica, or Erasmus, or Stephens thirteen centuries later, when moulding the Textus Receptus.'"*

In other words, Dr. Scrivener is saying that there were corruptions so grievous in the earliest days (within 100 years after the New Testament was written) that the manuscripts that were the purest were **not** the ones that Irenaeus had in 150 A.D., but the ones that Stunica, Erasmus, and Stephens had when formulating the Textus Receptus thirteen centuries later. Dan Wallace misquoted Dr. Scrivener's position on heretical corruption of the Greek New Testament.

Byzantine Manuscripts and the KJB

#148 Issue: Dan Wallace agreed that it was the "Byzantine Manuscripts" that stood behind the King James Bible. (Script, p. 32)

Comment by Dr. Waite: These Byzantine Manuscripts are called the Traditional Text or the Textus Receptus or the Received Text which has been historically accepted by the churches from the Apostolic Age down to this present day. By the way, 99% of the over 5,255 Greek manuscripts that we have in existence today, stand for the King James Bible (5,210). Only B, ℵ (Vatican and Sinai) and 43 followers stand with the Westcott and Hort type manuscripts that underlie the new versions. This is less than 1% of the manuscripts we have today! The data for these figures comes from Dr. Jack Moorman's excellent book, *Forever Settled.* It is **B.F.T. #1428**, 217 large pages, @ $21 +P&H.

John 1:18--Not Only Begotten "God"

#149 Issue: Kenneth Barker, speaking of John 1:18, wrongly says that this is a "clear statement of Christ as God." (Script, p. 32)

Comment by Dr. Waite: This is rather an acceptance of the Arian and Gnostic idea that Christ was a created being, and one of the "gods" thus created. This idea that the Lord Jesus Christ in John 1:18 should rightly be called the "only begotten GOD" (as the NASV does) is an absolute error. First of all, it is a manuscript error because there is not sufficient manuscript evidence to support it. Just because B and ℵ might have it does not mean it's true. The bulk of the manuscript evidence is definitely in favor of "only begotten SON" as pointed out above in **#143 Issue**. Secondly, to say the Lord Jesus is the "only begotten GOD" would mean that God could be begotten. God can't be begotten, He always was and always will be. This is a serious heretical Gnostic error.

#150 Issue: Kenneth Barker's NIV paraphrase of "only begotten" as "one and only" is in error. (Script, p. 33)

Comment by Dr. Waite: Kenneth Barker's New International Version has paraphrased its own Greek text. It is not an accurate translation at all. There are many added words in order to get around what they know is a problem in saying that the Lord Jesus Christ is the "only begotten GOD." He is God. He is God the Son. He is also God's "only begotten SON." He is NOT the Gnostic created "only begotten GOD."

#151 Issue: Dr. Chambers insisted on "only begotten Son" rather than "only begotten GOD." (Script, p. 33)

Comment by Dr. Waite: I would agree. The Lord Jesus Christ <u>is</u> the only begotten Son of God . This expression is used many places in our King James Bible.

#152 Issue: Dr. Chambers gave a good stiff answer to James White. He said: "I do understand the only begotten Son." (Script, p. 33)

Comment by Dr. Waite: Dr. Chambers rose to defend strongly the Lord Jesus Christ as the "only begotten Son." He is to be commended.

#153 Issue: Know-it-all James White scolded Dr. Chambers by saying: "You have to look at what the manuscript states." (Script, p. 33)

Comment by Dr. Waite: The proper Greek manuscript does NOT state "only begotten GOD." It says "only begotten SON." The manuscripts have all be listed back in **#143 Issue** above. The reader is requested to refer back to that listing.

#154 Issue: Arthur Farstad said: "Well, I don't remember the exact number on each thing (on John 1:18)." Then he told Dr. Chambers, "they're saying that the *oldest* have only begotten GOD." (Script, p. 33)

Comment by Dr. Waite: Are ℵ and B the best because they are the oldest? No, they are among the very worst because they were corrupted by heretics. This is what Dr. Strouse was getting at. They were corrupted by Gnostics in Egypt. The Egyptian Gnostics changed the documents in many ways. I believe that these Gnostics made most of the changes in the Textus Receptus of the 5,604 places by actual count where there is a difference. That is the distinction between the Westcott and Hort Greek text of 1881 and our Textus Receptus that underlies our King James Bible. In the 5,604 places, where the Egyptian heretics and Gnostics made most of these changes, there are a total of 9,970 Greek words. This is 30 words short of 10,000 words that have been altered from the Textus Receptus. They have either added words that **weren't** there, or subtracted words that **were** there or **changed** the words in some other way.

Lesbian Mollenkott, Sodomy & NIV

#155 Issue: John Ankerberg brought up the removal of sodomy from the NIV. (Script, p. 34)

Comment by Dr. Waite: It is true that every reference to sodomy or sodomites is gone from the New International Version. Kenneth Barker can say it is not due to the lesbian, Virginia Mollenkott, or some other particular person if he wants, but this fact is true. I maintain that it was lesbian Mollenkott (who hates these words) who saw to it that they were removed!

#156 Issue: Kenneth Barker said: "[In the early 1970's], Virginia Mollenkott was consulted briefly and only in a minor way on matters of English style." (Script, p. 34)

Comment by Dr. Waite: Kenneth Barker is evading the truth by peddling both half truths and outright falsehood! This is deplorable! Kenneth Barker made a false statement at this point. Dr. Chambers is going to answer that it is false. It was not simply "in a minor way." She was an English stylist consultant and her involvement was "in a major way." We have seven different titles dealing with Virginia Mollenkott. We offer a tape of an interview with Virginia Mollenkott and Mrs. Waite. It is **B.F.T. #697 @ $4.00 +P&H**. This tape was made years ago before Mrs. Mollenkott announced her lesbianism publicly. Mrs. Waite asked her straight out, "are you a lesbian?" Virginia Mollenkott said she would not answer that question. She said: "If I say yes that would alienate my straight friends, and if I say no that would alienate my gay friends."

Before this tape I wrote an answer to her book, *Women, Men, and the Bible*. It is **B.F.T. #518**, 39 pages @ **$4 +P&H**. I refuted her terrible denunciation of the Lord Jesus Christ. She portrays Jesus as one that is half male and half female and various other things. This is a terrible theological error. The New International Version committee had available to them Virginia Mollenkott's book, *Women, Men, and the Bible*. I knew Virginia Mollenkott while she was teaching at Shelton College. I was a visiting professor of Speech at that time. I was on the same campus at Ringwood, New Jersey, with Virginia Mollenkott as a fellow teacher. Mrs. Mollenkott was full time in English and was a lesbian at that time. She had lesbian activities with various girls in the school and she was asked to leave because of it.

A third analysis we have (**B.F.T. #2319**, 15 large pages, @ **$1.50 + P&H**) is entitled, *Lesbian Mollenkott out of the Closet*. Then **B.F.T. #2439 @ $4.00** is a cassette tape of an interview with Virginia Mollenkott by Dr. Joseph Chambers, who is one of the men on this telecast. We also have **B.F.T. #2439-P @ $3.00 +**

P&H. This is thirty pages in length. Mrs. Waite analyzes that interview and adds some more things to it. She transcribes the entire interview by Dr. Chambers. **B.F.T. #2490/8 @ $4.00 + P&H** is a tape by Mrs. Waite concerning Mollenkott's part in the NIV and lesbian. **B.F.T. #2491 @ $4.00 +P&H** is also a tape by Mrs. Waite. So, when Dr. Kenneth Barker says that nothing was known of her lesbian views you can see that this is a false statement. There are many things that were known about her lesbian activities that he could have checked into.

#157 Issue: Kenneth Barker, you remember, tried to down-play Mollenkott's part in the NIV. (Script, p. 34)

Comment by Dr. Waite: Virginia Mollenkott was not only a consultant of English style, but in the early parts of the advertisements for the New International Version she was called one of the "translators" and one of the "editors." I read from one of the early advertisements about the New International Version. I see that in the listing they state:

> *"The following is a partial list of these scholars although the scores of translators and editors come from many different denominations. . . . "*

The governing body is given. Kenneth Barker is the head of it. He graduated from Dallas Theological Seminary (Th.M., 1960). The advertisement continued:

> *"The following is a partial list of these scholars. Many other critics have assisted the process that are not here named."*

The very top of this advertisement is captioned: **"The Translators.** Names in that list is Virginia Mollenkott of William Patterson College. You can see that she is listed as a **"translator"** by the NIV. This advertisement piece has various headings such as: "The **Translators,** the Translation Process, The Reviews, the Choice of Editions." Kenneth Barker should not be surprised if Virginia Mollenkott has been called a "**translator**" by some, given the printed advertisements to that effect.

#158 Issue: Kenneth Barker said, speaking of Virginia Mollenkott, "at that time, she had the reputation of being a committed evangelical Christian with expertise in contemporary English idiom and usage." (Script, p. 34)

Comment by Dr. Waite: No, Dr. Barker, Virginia Mollenkott had the reputation of being a committed apostate as well as a wicked, sinful, practicing lesbian homosexual! She may have had "expertise in contemporary English idiom and usage," but she was **not** a "committed evangelical Christian." If you would read, *Women, Men, and The Bible,* as I have reviewed it and commented on it in a lengthy paper, you would see she was anything but a "committed evangelical Christian." After reading that book it makes you wonder if she was even saved. She came from a Plymouth Brethren background, attended Bob Jones University, but the way she phrases certain things, you wonder if she is even a Christian much less a "committed evangelical Christian." I believed as I reviewed her book that she was lost. She is a member of the apostate-led Episcopal Church which is a member of the apostate National Council of Churches. She writes like an apostate.

#159 Issue: Kenneth Barker also said of Mollenkott: "Nothing was known of her lesbian views." (Script, p. 34)

    Comment by Dr. Waite: It is not only a question of her "lesbian views"; it is also her **lesbian activities**. Kenneth Barker is trying once more to downplay the wickedness of this woman. It is not my fault that Kenneth Barker and the NIV Committee did not know of Mollenkott's lesbian activities. These activities were known long before the 1970's. We have in **B.F.T.** #2319 (15 large pages @ **$1.50 + P&H**) her biographical sketch. This was sent to us by Abington Press which was the publisher of *Women, Men, and the Bible*. I wrote to Abington Press. Mary Ellen Wrist of their department of Advertising and Publicity, on March 27, 1977, sent me what Virginia Mollenkott had been doing. This was in her own handwriting. She is professor of English and department chairman of English at William Patterson College of Wayne, NJ. She was chairman of the English Department at Shelton College from 1955-1963. Nyack College from 1963-1967. She was born in Philadelphia and lived there from 1932-1955. She lived in Ringwood, NJ from 1955-1956. She lived in Hewittt, NJ from 1970 and following Apparently, this is where she is now living. She was at Shelton College for nine years

    I was there as professor and teacher probably in 1961 or 1962 shortly before she left. I flew in once a week on a Wednesday. I was pastor at Faith Baptist Church in Newton, Massachusetts. Dr McIntire was the President of the board of the school. He wanted me to teach there and paid for my air fare each week. He wanted to use my Ph.D. to help with his accreditation problems at the college. Virginia Mollenkott was there in the 1950's and early 1960's. I knew of her lesbian activities at that particular time. The President, Clyde Kennedy, died suddenly. The President who was going to be taking over, Dr. Arthur Steele, said he would not be President of this school while Virginia Mollenkott was on the teaching staff. Dr. McIntire fired her and told her not to return. Virginia Mollenkott was married at that time to Fred Mollenkott who was a fine Christian man. I wrote Dr. Steele on March 22, 1977. He answered my letter and verified these facts.

    I also have in **B.F.T.** #2319, a letter from Dr. Bob Jones Jr., the Chancellor of Bob Jones University, which states:

> *"Archer Weniger tells me you have a booklet on Virginia Raimey Mollenkott. I would appreciate you sending me a copy together with the bill. We had a definite problem with her because she insisted on hobnobbing with a few girls when she was employed as a teacher here for one year __in the 1950's__."*

Here going way back to the 1950's we see that Bob Jones University had a problem with Virginia Mollenkott's lesbian activities. The actual testimony of Virginia Mollenkott's coming "out of the closet" is published in *The Witness* in June of 1991, on page 20. It was entitled "Church Needs New Sexual Ethic, an interview with Carol Carter Hayward and Virginia Ramey Mollenkott." In the interview she says that she had been a lesbian for many years. In fact, she said she has been a lesbian practically all her life. She says on page 22:

> *"My lesbianism was always very much a part of me. I tried to be*
> *a heterosexual. I married myself off, but when I did, ultimately*
> *what I realized was that God created me as I was."*

She blames God's creation for her lesbianism. This is unscriptural. The sin of homosexual lesbian, like all other sins, is a **LEARNED ACTIVITY**. God never made a lesbian homosexual!

#160 Issue: Kenneth Barker said: "I don't see how anyone could say that we watered down homosexual and lesbian practices. . . ." (Script, p. 35)

Comment by Dr. Waite: Virginia Mollenkott was the one that said the New International translating committee watered down some of these practices. She said that "homosexual offenders" could mean those who were "homophobic" or who offend homosexuals as well as referring to homosexuals themselves. In fact, there is a law suit, I'm told, that is now underway against the Oxford University Press because of the King James Bible that they publish. This law suit is put forth by the ACLU (American Civil Liberties Union). They are trying to get the King James Bible to cease publication because of its condemnation of homosexuals and sodomites. There is no law suit against the NIV and its phrasing of these sins.

#161 Issue: Kenneth Barker said of his NIV: "There are some places where sodomy is translated homosexuality." (Script, p. 35)

Comment by Dr. Waite: That is not an accurate statement at all. Dr. Barker has said there are some **"places"** (plural) where sodomy is translated homosexuality. There is only **one** place in the entire NIV (according to their exhaustive concordance) where sodomy is translated, NOT "homosexuality," but "homosexual offenders." That is the problem that Dr. Chambers skillfully brought up. The NIV does not specifically say "homosexuality" or "homosexuals" at all. It says "homosexual offenders." "Those who offend homosexuals" is a valid interpretation of the NIV's paraphrase of 1 Corinthians 6:9. For Dr. Kenneth Barker to say on this telecast that there are some **"places"** in the NIV "where sodomy is translated homosexuality" is absolutely false.

#162 Issue: Kenneth Barker said: "But, don't forget all the other Hebrew words that are not those words that are translated homosexuality." (Script, p. 36)

Comment by Dr. Waite: Again, he uses the plural word, **"words"** implying that there are many references to "homosexuality." There is **only one place** in the whole NIV where the word "homosexual" is used. This one place is 1 Corinthians 6:9 where it says "homosexual offenders" which is interpreted by lesbian Virginia Mollenkott as "those who offend homosexuals."

Still More From James White

#163 Issue: James White said: "I hope everyone notices that the King James Only advocates will always use terms like 'changed.,' 'deleted,' so on and so forth."(Script, p. 36)

Comment by Dr. Waite: Why does he say "The King James Only" advocates? Why doesn't he also say the New American Standard Only advocates, or the New International Only advocates, or the New King James Only advocates, or the Revised Standard Only advocates? Why is it **just** the King James Only advocates?

#164 Issue: James White said: "God does not call us to argue in circles." (Script, p. 36)

Comment by Dr. Waite: The foregoing argument was **not** "arguing in circles" where they say that the word "sodomite" is changed in the NIV. It **is** changed to "shrine prostitutes." That is very clear. There **has** been a change. Why does James White call that circular argumentation? We are talking about a standard. In 1611 A.D. the standard came out and was first translated. We call it the Authorized Version. This Authorized Version came out of England, out of the Anglican Church, during the reign of King James. This is why it is also called the King James Version. That was a standard. What does the "new kid on the block" have to say about that standard. Did the New International Version in 1972 when it was completed (according to Dr. Barker) change "sodomy" or not? Did they delete "sodomite" or did they not delete "sodomite"? They certainly **did** change "sodomy" and **did** delete "sodomite." There is nothing circular about that.

#165 Issue: James White said: "it would be just as easy for me to sit back and say 'Well, the King James doesn't say anything about homosexuality.'" (Script, p. 36)

Comment by Dr. Waite: The NIV doesn't say anything about homosexuality either! Why does he bring that up. The King James Bible uses "sodomites" several times. This is certainly "homosexuality." The NIV only uses "homosexual offenders" once in the entire NIV.

VII.
COMMENTS ON PROGRAMS #7-#8
Script, Pages 37-55

The Bible Issue Divides Churches

#166 Issue: Samuel Gipp said of a church that uses the NIV: "I don't know that you can remain under that ministry." (Script, p. 37)

Comment by Dr. Waite: Well, I would agree with that. I wouldn't want to go to a church where the minister preaches from the New International Version. This is a false and unreliable version.

#167 Issue: Kenneth Barker talked on and on without letting anyone else enter in, and John Ankerberg let him. (Script, p. 37)

Comment by Dr. Waite: Notice how Kenneth Barker is given another **11 inches** of space on the script to express his viewpoint. Where is the fairness for the King James Bible side?

#168 Issue: In regard to those using the NIV or a non-King James Bible, Kenneth Barker said: "I don't think this is an important enough issue to divide a church over." (Script, p. 37)

Comment by Dr. Waite: If the Bible isn't an important issue for Dr. Kenneth Barker to divide a church over then what is? I don't know of another issue more important than the Word of God. If it divides a church, let it divide. The church should stand for the King James Bible. I suppose that if they stand for the NIV then they should all get together and have an NIV church, or an NASV church or an RSV church. We ought to have a unity it would appear, even though they are using other than the proper King James Bible.

#169 Issue: Kenneth Barker agreed that each church should decide which version to use and stick to it to avoid confusion. (Script, p. 37)

Comment by Dr. Waite: I would agree with that statement. In many churches in years past I think the decision has been made time and time again that they would use the King James Bible. In recent years, the decision has been made, either by the Pastor or the entire church, in some churches, to take the New International version as the Bible for their church and they have thrown out the King James. In some cases, this is in spite of the church's rules to use only the King James Bible. There is a church in our area that is affiliated with the General Associated of Regular Baptist Churches (GARBC) that decided to reach a compromise between the King James Bible and the New International Version. That church has placed an NIV/KJB parallel version in the pews.

Manuscripts Since KJB Are Not Used

#170 Issue: Kenneth Barker referred to the manuscripts discovered since 1611 when the King James Bible was translated. (Script, p. 37)

Comment by Dr. Waite: The last part of this comment where Kenneth Barker says:

> *"If you take into account **all of the Greek manuscripts and papyri** that have been discovered since 1611 when the King James translators did their work, . . ."*

My friend, this sounds like the NIV and the NASV have taken into account "all the Greek manuscripts and papyri that have been discovered since 1611." That is just plain false and misleading in the extreme. Did you know that, in fact, the New International Version, the New American Standard Version, and the other new versions of our day take into account only two basic manuscripts (B, and ℵ the Vatican and Sinai manuscripts) and perhaps 43 other manuscripts that agree with B and ℵ? They let over 5,210 Greek manuscripts go begging because they are unified in their testimony and testify in favor of the Textus Receptus readings. These versions just set them aside since they are a part of the so-called Majority text, or the so-called Textus Receptus type, or the so- called Syrian text, or the so-called Traditional Text. They just considered these manuscripts to be of none effect. They have ignored over 99% of all the evidence. They are only using less than 1% of what God has preserved for us. This is a correction that needs to be made at this point.

NASV not a "Literal Translation" as KJB

#171 Issue: Don Wilkins agreed with Kenneth Barker that the New American Standard Version was "a literal translation." (Script, p. 38)

Comment by Dr. Waite: That is false. It is not a word-for-word, "literal translation." I have found in my research of the New American Standard Version (**B.F.T. #1494-P,** 187 large pages, @ **$15.00** + P&H) over **4,000** examples of non-literal translation (dynamic equivalency). Compared to the original Hebrew and Greek texts, they have added to God's Words, subtracted from God's Words, or changed God's Words in some other way. I disagree with that statement completely and totally.

So-Called "Best" Manuscripts Not "Best"

#172 Issue: Don Wilkins, of the NASV, said: "We still expect the best words or the best readings to be in the best manuscripts and we operate that way." (Script, p. 38)

Comment by Dr. Waite: He means B and ℵ when he talks about "the best manuscripts." Dean Burgon has pointed out and proved that B and ℵ are the foulest manuscripts that have ever seen the light of day.

The "Canons" of Textual Criticism

#173 Issue: John Ankerberg says that textual criticism just follows some of the "rules" they have laid down. (Script, p. 38)

Comment by Dr. Waite: Let's pause right here and look at a few of the rules or "canons" of textual criticism. Those principles were principles laid down originally by Westcott and Hort in 1881 in their *Introduction to the Greek Text*. They were principles that made it look like B and ℵ (Vatican and Sinai manuscripts) were the best. These rules were made after they decided that B (Vatican) was the best manuscript. The Vatican or B is really one of the worst. They said the shortest was always the best. Well, B (the Vatican) is the shortest, therefore that's the best, right? No, wrong, it's still the worst. Another of their rules was to take the most difficult reading. B (the Vatican) has the most difficult, ungrammatical readings, therefore that's the best, right? No, wrong, it's still the worst. This is certainly circular reasoning that James White talked about above. I could make up some "canons" or rules that would point toward the Textus Receptus, also. Anyone can play that game.

#174 Issue: Dan Wallace said: "I would agree with the text behind these modern translations." (Script, p. 38)

Comment by Dr. Waite: The text behind the modern translations is the most error-ridden text that ever could be found. Dean Burgon said it was the worst text that had ever seen the light of day. It is based upon Westcott and Hort's false text of B and ℵ. This man, Dan Wallace, who claims to have spent "hundreds of hours" in the field of textual criticism was in the wrong field as far as I'm concerned. He's come up with the exact opposite view that truth would dictate. For twenty two years I was favorable to the Textus Receptus enemies. I tacitly agreed with all those arguments against it. I was with the Westcott and Hort men.

For many years I didn't even know there was a Textus Receptus. They didn't teach us that at Dallas Theological Seminary. They were not educating us as far as the Greek manuscripts, even though I majored in New Testament Literature and Exegesis. I can't believe as a Master of Theology (taking four graduate years of classroom study), they never opened the arguments once about the Textus Receptus or told us there was such a thing. They gave us a one-sided lop-sided view of New

Testament Greek. Dan Wallace, after alleged "hundreds of hours? is now in favor of the Greek text of the modern translations (the Westcott and Hort kind of text). I've spent hundreds of hours in the last twenty five years of studying, reading, and reproducing documents and manuscripts. We have over 1,000 titles defending the King James Bible and the Hebrew and Greek text that underlies it. We believe that our standard Greek text that underlies our King James Bible is the proper text and the only text that we should use; not the text of these modern translations that Dan Wallace is pushing.

#175 Issue: Dan Wallace said: "Choose the reading that best explains the rise of the others." (Script, p. 38)

Comment by Dr. Waite: The principal of looking at the reading that explains the others is the false way of looking at manuscript evidence. Looking for what explains the other readings is a subjective view of evidence. It is not evidence, it is guess work. This is one of the principles that was laid down by Westcott and Hort in their *Introduction to the Greek New Testament* , when they came out with their false Greek text that underlies the English Revised Version of 1881. This was a text that had been worked on by Westcott and Hort for about twenty years. It was a secret Greek text. Nobody on the translating committee was to breathe a word of this text until after 1881 when it was published.

Finally, Dean John William Burgon got hold of that text. In 1883 (two years later) he completed a series of articles in the *Quarterly Review.* In these three articles, Dean Burgon analyzed: (1) the false English Revised Version compared to the King James Bible; (2) the false Greek text of Westcott and Hort; and (3) the false theory behind that Greek text of Westcott and Hort. In the Dean Burgon Society in their 1996 meeting in Massachusetts, it was decided to reprint *The Revision Revised* of Dean John William Burgon. It is now available from the DBS and the Bible For Today in a beautiful hard back gold-covered edition. There are 640 pages in that book. It is **B.F.T. #611 @ $25.00 +P&H.** When Dan Wallace says he is going to look at the external data including Greek manuscripts, this is not the case. These men do not even look at the Greek manuscripts. These men are not being honest when they say they look at **all** of the Greek manuscripts.

Do you know how many Greek manuscripts God has preserved for us (according to Kurt Aland in 1967)? We have 5,255 Greek manuscripts. Do you know how many manuscripts these Westcott and Hort followers really look at and use? They look at B and ℵ (Vatican and Sinai) and about 43 other manuscripts that follow B and ℵ. Is that looking at **all** the Greek manuscripts? This is less than 1% of the evidence (45 is less than 1% of 5,255). What is the basis of the Textus Receptus that underlies our King James Bible? This Greek text has about 5,210 manuscripts behind it. This is over 99% of the evidence. Don't believe it when Dan Wallace says he is going to look at **all** the manuscripts. They basically look at one--B, the Vatican manuscript. Then Dan Wallace says he looked at non-Greek manuscripts, including *"the Latin, the Coptic, the Ethiopic, all the rest, and it also involves looking at Church Fathers."* Many of these versions don't line up as well either with the Westcott and Hort type of text in many instances.

As far as "looking at the Church Fathers," Dean Burgon exhaustively went into the Church Fathers and their quotations or allusions to the New Testament. Church Fathers were pastors, bishops, and church leaders of that early day. There were about three hundred church fathers that wrote extensively. Dean Burgon and his staff amassed over 86,000 quotations or allusions to the Greek New Testament or the Latin New Testament of their day. Dean Burgon found that not only were a majority of the Greek quotations or allusions to the Scriptures based on Textus Receptus type of quotations, but also they were in a majority of **three to two**. This is 60% to 40% in favor of the text that underlies our King James Bible. Dean Burgon referred to this as the Traditional Text.

Dr. Jack Moorman, in his recent study on the Church Fathers and what they really showed, found that an even greater percentage of the early Church Fathers' quotations of the Scripture were Textus Receptus type quotations. He found the ratio of about 70% to 30% in favor of the TR over against the B and א text. His study is called *Early Church and the Authorized Version--a Demonstration.* It is **B.F.T. #2136**, 63 large pages @ **$6.00** + P&H.

#176 Issue: Dan Wallace said: "The earlier manuscripts would be preferred over the later ones." (Script, p. 38)

Comment by Dr. Waite: Dan Wallace is now giving a second Westcott and Hort rule in finding out which is the "best" reading. First he says to take the text that explains the rise of the others. Then Dan Wallace says, *"The earlier manuscripts would be preferred over the later ones."* This is all right unless the earlier manuscripts have been tampered with, and that's the case here. They have been tampered with. The earlier manuscripts were not as reliable as the later ones because of the heretics that tampered with them. Notice again a quote from Dean Burgon's book, *The Revision Revised*, page 30. He is referring to Dr. Frederick H. Scrivener, one of the members who was on the revision committee for the English Revised Version (ERV) of 1881. He stood for the Traditional Text and against the text of Westcott and Hort. He wrote:

> *"The worst corruptions to which the New Testament has ever been subjected originated, within a hundred years after it had been composed: that Irenaeus [A.D. 150] and the African Fathers, and the whole Western, with a portion of the Syrian Church, used far inferior manuscripts to those employed by Stunica, or Erasmus, or Stephens thirteen centuries later, when moulding the Textus Receptus."*

Dr. Scrivener has given us the reason why we can say that many of the earliest manuscripts were corrupted by heretics. The church almost immediately rejected

B and ℵ and those forty three manuscripts that went along with them. They expressed their rejection by ceasing to copy them. On the contrary, the churches accepted the manuscripts that agree with the present 5,210 manuscripts plus when they molded the Textus Receptus. Remember, I have already mentioned that B and ℵ were very bad manuscripts. Notice what Dean Burgon said in *The Revision Revised* on page 16:

> "... *ℵ, B, and D* are three of *the most scandalously corrupt copies extant;*--exhibit the most shamefully *mutilated texts* which are anywhere to be met with:--have become, by whatever process (for their history is wholly unknown), the depositories of the largest amount of *fabricated readings, ancient blunders and intentional perversions of Truth,*--which are discoverable in any known copies of the Word of God."

#177 Issue: Dan Wallace said, regarding the earlier manuscripts are the best, "Even Dean Burgon himself acknowledged that." (Script, p. 38)

Comment by Dr. Waite: Dean Burgon said only if these earlier manuscripts were not tampered with, were not corrupted, and no heretical corrections had been made, then, and only then, the earlier dated manuscript would be preferred. Otherwise, that rule does not apply. "Antiquity" is one of the Dean Burgon's "seven notes of truth." But when the earlier ones have been corrupted as Dr. Scrivener's quote and Dean Burgon explained, then the older is **not** better. Dean Burgon would be upset with this deliberate misquotation of his views. Here is what Dean Burgon wrote in his book, *The Causes of the Corruption of the Traditional Text* on this point of "antiquity."

> "Nothing of the sort, I answer. The direct reverse is the case. Our appeal is always made to antiquity; and it is nothing else but a truism to assert that the oldest reading is also the best. . . .

> "The characteristic note, the one distinguishing feature, of all the monstrous and palpable perversions of the text of Scripture just now under considerations this:--that they are never vouched for by the oldest documents generally, but only by a few of them,--two, three, or more of the oldest documents being observed as a rule to yield conflicting testimony, (which in this subject-matter is in fact contradictory). In this way the oldest witnesses nearly always refute one another, and indeed dispose of one another's evidence almost as often as that evidence is untrustworthy." [Dean Burgon, *The Causes of the Corruption of the Traditional Text of the Holy Gospels*, pp. 194-195]

This book is available as **B.F.T. #1159**, about 400 pages, @ **$15.00 + P&H**. It is due out in hardback sometime in 1998. It is a very good work by Dean John William Burgon and should be in every Christian's library.

Earliest Manuscripts Not Always Best

#178 Issue: Dan Wallace said: "And so we want to look at the earliest manuscripts because you're going to have less time between the time of the original till you get to those early copies.". (Script, p. 38)

Comment by Dr. Waite: Again, you would go to the "earliest" manuscripts only if these oldest manuscripts had not been corrupted. Just take Mark 16:9-20 as an example. You should get Dean Burgon's book, *The Last Twelve Verses of Mark*. It is **B.F.T. #1139**, 400 pages, perfect bound for **$15.00** + P&H. Basically, the only two manuscripts in Dean Burgon's day that rejected Mark 16:9-20 were B and ℵ. Yet B and ℵ are the "earliest manuscripts" from the standpoint of the substance on which they were copied. They are far from the "earliest" witnesses, however. The evidence is strong against B and ℵ and in favor of the last twelve verses of Mark.

Here is the evidence offered by Dean Burgon: 18 other uncials have Mark 16:9-20. About 600 cursive copies have Mark 16:9-20. Every Lectionary of the East has Mark 16:9-20. 10 ancient versions have Mark 16:9-20. Over half of these 10 versions pre-date B and ℵ. 19 quotations from early Church Fathers quote or allude to Mark 16:9-20. Over half of these quotations pre-date B and ℵ. All of them prove that B and ℵ were wrong in rejecting the last twelve verses of Mark. B and ℵ may be a **part** of antiquity, but they are not **all** of antiquity.

TR Greek Has Geographical Distribution

#179 Issue: Dan Wallace said: "You have geographical distribution--very important principles. (Script, p. 38)

Comment by Dr. Waite: In the Greek texts that underlie these modern versions and perversions (namely B, ℵ and company) you don't have geographical distribution at all. You have one narrow source--Egypt. Do you call that "geographical distribution"? The Textus Receptus **does** have geographical distribution from all over the then-known-world (from Asia Minor, Palestine, Italy and more).

#180 Issue: Dan Wallace said: "You've got geographical distribution in the early centuries." (Script, p. 39)

Comment by Dr. Waite: That's not what the new versions do. They don't have geographical distribution. They don't have manuscripts from Italy, Carthage, and Antioch. For instance in *The Last Twelve Verses of Mark*, Dean Burgon has an illustration of what we are talking about here. The only two manuscripts in Dean Burgon's day that didn't have the last twelve verses of Mark were B and ℵ. What about the ones that **do** have the last twelve verses of Mark?

What about the Church Fathers who quoted from the last twelve verses of Mark? What about the ten ancient versions that contained the last twelve verses of Mark? These include Peshitto Syriac, the Vetus Itala (Old Latin), the Curetonian Syriac, the Thebaic (Sahidic) Egyptian, the Memphitic (Coptic) Egyptian, the Gothic of Ulphilas, the Latin Vulgate, the Philoxenian Syriac, the Ethiopic, and the Georgian)? Those ten ancient versions came from all over the then-known-world. This is **real** geographic distribution. What about the nineteen Church Fathers who quote from Mark 16:9-20? Over half of these Church Fathers quoted from these verses **before** B and ℵ ever saw the light of day. These nineteen Church Fathers were: Papias 100 A.D., Justin Martyr 151 A.D., Irenaeus 180 A.D., Hippolytus 200 A.D., Vincentius 256 A.D., Acta Pilati 250 A.D., Apostolical Constitutions 200's-300's A.D., Eusebius 325 A.D., Marinus 325 A.D., Aphraates The Persian 337 A.D., Ambrose 374-397 A.D., Chrysostom 400 A.D., Jerome 331-420 A.D., Augustine 395-430 A.D., Nestorius 430 A.D., Cyril of Alexandria 430 A.D., Victor of Antioch 425 A.D., Hesychius 500 A.D., and Synopsis Scripturae Sacrae 500's A.D. It would have been statistically impossible to have had all of these witnesses quoting the exact words of Mark 16:9-20 without having an accurate copy of these words in their hands--a copy that came directly from the original Gospel of Mark.

John 5:4 Defended

#181 Issue: In talking about the Greek text of John 5:4, Dan Wallace said: "We have to look at what is the scribe more likely to do." (Script, p. 39)

Comment by Dr. Waite: That is foolish speculation. You don't ask yourself, what would the scribe have done in copying a portion of Scripture hundreds of years ago. That's what Westcott and Hort called "transcriptional probability." This is subjective to the nth degree. This is not sound textual criticism. In sound textual criticism you take the **facts**. You don't attempt to speculate as to what a scribe **might** have done or might not have done. This is one of the fallacies of Westcott and Hort's *Introduction to the Greek New Testament* of 1881.

Let's look at John 5:4 for documentary manuscripts. Dr. Jack Moorman has written, *Early Manuscripts and the Authorized Version--A Closer Look with Manuscript Digest and Summaries,* (**B.F.T. #1825**, 157 pages @ **$15.00 + P&H**). In this book, on page 102, you see the external evidence in favor of the TR/KJB reading for John 5:3-4. The words from the King James Bible say,

"In these lay a great multitude of impotent folk, of blind, halt, withered, waiting for the moving of the water. For an angel went down at a certain season into the pool, and troubled the water: whosoever then first after the troubling of the water stepped in was made whole of whatsoever disease he had."

Dr. Moorman, in his *Early Manuscripts,* page 102, gives the manuscript evidence

against and **for** these two verses. The evidence against this verse is slight: It includes: papyrus 66 and 75, ℵ and B, uncials C*, D, W-supplement, 0125, 0141, pc, d, flg, Vulgate-pt, Curetonian Syriac, sa, bo-pt, ach2, Armenian-mss. What about the favorable evidence for this verse: uncials: A, C-3, E, F, G, H, K, L, M, (S), U, V, X-comm., Gamma, Delta, Theta, Lambda, Psi, 047, 063, 078.. Cursives : MAJORITY, family 1 and 13. The Old Latin: a, aur, b, c, e, ff2, g1, j, r1. The Syriac: Peshitto, Harclian, Palestinian. Coptic: bo-pt, ; Armenian, Ethiopic. Also extant in Y, Omega, 055, 0211,0233?. Dr. Moorman states:

> *"Verse seven pre-supposes a miraculous moving of the water. Tertullian (c. 200 A.D.) refers to the passage. Tatian (c. 175 A.D.) placed it in his Diatessaron. The account illustrates the `long time' (verse 6) that man with misplaced faith (angels, water) will have to wait."* (Loc. cit.)

How can Dan Wallace say that the scribe saw this verse in the margin. This is pure speculation and gross error on his part.

More So-Called "Canons" of Criticism

#182 Issue: Dan Wallace said: "They're more likely to add than to omit." (Script, p. 39)

Comment by Dr. Waite: This is another false statement. The very opposite is true. Statistical research on the mistakes of those who copy documents has shown that when people copy things, they tend to **omit** material. They do **not** tend to **add** material. Their eye goes down to the next line below and they miss a whole line of thought. The Westcott-Hort, B/ℵ Greek text has **omitted** no less than **2,886** Greek words, according to Dr. Moorman's actual count. Most of those omissions were purposeful rather than merely accidental.

#183 Issue: Dan Wallace said: "What is the author likely to have done?" (Script, p. 39)

Comment by Dr. Waite: I think he means "writer" here. God was the "Author" of the Bible, not any human beings. Here you have the very speculative guess as to what the writers of Scripture actually wrote. Here is what you call, in the Westcott and Hort's false theory, the "intrinsic probability." In other words, what would the writers such as Paul, Peter, James, John and the others have written? This is false speculation. It is pure guesswork. No one on earth can predict accurately what the writers **might** have written. You must deal exclusively with what they **did** write. There are three things by which the Lord has secured the accuracy of His Word: manuscripts, ancient versions, and quotations by the Church Fathers. We don't need guess work. In fact, we must reject it totally!

Is NASV Closest to Hebrew & Greek?

#184 Issue: Speaking of the New American Standard Version, John

Ankerberg said: "It's the most accurate to what the Greek or Hebrew word was." (Script, p. 39)

Comment by Dr. Waite: This is absolutely false. The King James Bible is the most accurate English translation of the Bible. For documentary proof of over 4,000 uses of dynamic equivalency in the NASV, please request my study entitled: *The New American Standard Version Analyzed and Refuted*. It is **B.F.T. #1494-P**, 187 large pages @ **$15.00 + $3.50 P&H**. It is a mystery how John Ankerberg can make such erroneous statements on television, on video tape, and in the transcript!

NASV and NIV Original Texts Similar

#185 Issue: Dan Wallace said: "In terms of the textual basis, the textual basis, the difference between New American Standard and NIV is minuscule." (Script, p. 39)

Comment by Dr. Waite: While it is true that the New American Standard Version and the New International Version's New Testament textual basis is almost the same, this textual basis is in error. I urge you to get my book, *Defending The King James Version*. I show very clearly that both the NASV and the NIV have false texts. They use the false Ben Asher text instead of the Ben Chayyim text for the Hebrew Old Testament. They use the false New Testament Greek text of Westcott and Hort (which is similar to the current Nestle-Aland 26th or 27th editions, and the United Bible Societies 3rd or 4th editions) instead of the Textus Receptus text.

NKJV & NASV Philosophy Similar?

#186 Issue: Dan Wallace said: "In terms of the translation philosophy between the *New King James* and the *New American Standard* it's not that great of a difference. (Script, p. 39)

Comment by Dr. Waite: The translation philosophy between the NKJV and the NASV, to a greater or lesser extent, **is** the same. They believe in dynamic equivalence! I have found over 4,000 examples of dynamic equivalence in the New American Standard Version and over 2,000 examples of dynamic equivalence in the New King James Version. These versions have either added to God's Words, subtracted from God's Words, or changed God's Words in some other way. These documented studies are available from the Bible for Today as **B.F.T. #1494-P ($15)** and **B.F.T. #1442 ($10)** respectively. The translation philosophies of the NASV and the NKJV differ in the **degree** of dynamic equivalency used.

"Words" Minimized

#187 Issue: Dan Wallace said that various translations such as NKJV and NASV and NIV "get to the attention of the reader so he understands exactly what that biblical author meant in the first place, whether it has the same words or not." (Script, p. 39)

Comment by Dr. Waite: *"Whether it has the same words or not?"* The New King James (over 2,000 times) didn't care if the words are the same. The New American Standard Version (over 4,000 times) didn't care that the same words were used. The New International Version (over 6,653 times--and I stopped counting) didn't care if the same words were used or not. When words are different, the meaning, no matter how slightly, cannot possibly be the same!

"Formal Equivalence" Falsely Defined

#188 Issue: Dan Wallace gave a false definition of "formal equivalence." (Script, p. 39)

Comment by Dr. Waite: He doesn't even know what "formal equivalence" means. It doesn't mean if you "have 17 words in Greek you're going to have 17 words in English." It simply means the **forms** of the words are to be equivalent wherever possible. Where did this man learn these things that are not true. "Formal equivalence" has to do with the **grammatical forms** of the words. If you have a noun in the Hebrew or Greek it should be translated into English, wherever possible, as a noun. If you have a verb form in the Hebrew or Greek you should bring it over into English wherever possible as a verb. That's formal equivalence. It is **not** to be understood as Dan Wallace implied, that is, having 17 words in Greek that must translate into 17 words in English. This is what you call a straw man's argument. You set up a straw man and then knock him down. The King James Bible has both **formal equivalence** and **verbal equivalence**. It pays attention to the **forms** of the words that God has given us in His original languages of Hebrew and Greek. The NKJV, NASV, NIV and others have not made this principle one of their basic tenets for translation.

Re-Arranging of Words

#189 Issue: Arthur Farstad said: "Even the *King James* has a lot of rearranging of words to make it beautiful English." (Script, p. 39)

Comment by Dr. Waite: The King James Bible has much **less** of this than these other versions do. The King James Bible keeps the forms of the words wherever possible. The Hebrew word order in Genesis 1:1 is: "In the beginning created God." In the Hebrew you quite often put the verb first and the subject second. In indicative sentences in English you put the subject first and the verb second. You have to change the order of the words here and there to adjust to the English, but the KJB does this much less frequently than either the NKJV, the NASV, or the NIV. As proof of this, the reader has only to consult the exhaustive analyses that I have done on the NKJV, NASV, and NIV as to their "dynamic equivalency."

Formal Equivalence Attacked

> **#190 Issue:** Dan Wallace said: "All translations have to get away from formal equivalency. (Script, p. 39)

     Comment by Dr. Waite: Why should they? If a proper definition of this term is used and understood, all of the translations should use "formal equivalency." He is using a wrong definition for "formal equivalence." He is confusing people with this false definition. The King James Bible nowhere attempted to use the same number of English words as were found in either the Hebrew or the Greek as Dan Wallace implies.

> **#191 Issue:** Dan Wallace commented that "Mary was with child" in the KJB was not a proper translation from the Greek text. (Script, p. 39)

     Comment by Dr. Waite: Dan Wallace refers to Matthew 1. He probably means Matthew 1:18. The Greek expression here is properly translated by the King James Bible as "with child." He is trying to make a case for his definition of formal equivalency which we have already explained is not the right definition.

NIV Editor Exalts Dynamic Equivalency

> **#192 Issue:** Kenneth Barker said: "All translations use dynamic equivalence. (Script, p. 40)

     Comment by Dr. Waite: While this may be true, that there are a very, very few examples of what Kenneth Barker might **call** "dynamic equivalence" in the King James Bible. Wherever the King James translators added words, they put those words in *italics* to show that the word does not appear in the Hebrew or the Greek but was added to convey the meaning for the English reader. For an example, in the New Testament the King James Bible has, "God forbid." This expression is found 9 times in the Old Testament and 15 times in the New Testament in the King James Bible. In the New Testament, the Greek is, *ou genoito* which literally translated would be "may it not be." In the 1611 sense, "God forbid" was an expression that adequately translated the Greek term. There are **very few** of these examples. Not so with the NKJV, NASV, or NIV. As for "dynamic equivalency," here's the score: My computer reports show more than 2,000 examples of dynamic equivalency in the New King James (**B.F.T. #1442 @ $10.00 +P&H**). I found more than 4,000 examples of dynamic equivalency in the New American Standard Version (**B.F.T. #1494-P @ $15.00 + P&H**). I found more than 6,653 examples of dynamic equivalency in the NIV (**B.F.T. #1749-P @ $25.00 + P&H**). The King James Bible shunned the technique of dynamic equivalency. Let the detractors find over 2,000, over 4,000, or over 6,653 examples in the King James Bible if they can. They cannot! This whole line of argument is a smoke screen in order to criticize the King James Bible and to justify these modern versions and perversions.

NIV Not A "Mediating Balance"

#193 Issue: Kenneth Barker, speaking of dynamic equivalency, said: "a mediating balance translation falling in the middle, such as the NIV." (Script, p. 40)

Comment by Dr. Waite: This is extremely false. The NIV is not a "mediating balance." It uses dynamic equivalency throughout its pages. In fact, dynamic equivalency is one of boasted principles used by the New International Version. The NIV may not have as many dynamic equivalences as are in the Living Version, but it is **not** a "balance" at all! My research discovered that the New International Version used dynamic equivalence in over 6,653 places.

Wonderful "Translations"?

#194 Issue: James White said, speaking of the NKJV, NASV, NIV and others: "We have the richest amount of wonderful, excellent translations available to us." (Script, p. 40)

Comment by Dr. Waite: These are **not** "wonderful, excellent translations." They are **paraphrases** to a greater or lesser extent.

#195 Issue: James White said: "We . . . have a number of excellent translations before us." (Script, p. 40)

Comment by Dr. Waite: I do not believe that the answer is to go ahead and look at all these translations of the Bible. These other translations (NKJV, NASV, NIV, and others) have numerous perversions of the Hebrew and the Greek. The only Bible that really gives what the Hebrew and the Greek has accurately said is the King James Bible.

#196 Issue: John Ankerberg said: "I don't believe that God protected the copyists." (Script, p. 41)

Comment by Dr. Waite: I **do** believe that, despite their human imperfections, God protected the copyists. He certainly has guarded His Word and to that extent He has kept His promise that He would preserve His Words. That includes His Providential care of the copyists.

What Percent Difference in Greek Texts?

#197 Issue: John Ankerberg asked what the two sides were "disagreeing on" as to the texts. Kenneth Barker said: "In the New Testament, less than 2%" (Script, p. 41)

Comment by Dr. Waite: That's an outright falsehood.

#198 Issue: Dr. Thomas Strouse said: "The Trinitarian Bible

Society has estimated it's about 7%." (Script, p. 41)

Comment by Dr. Waite: It was NOT the Trinitarian Bible Society that has come up with this figure. I was the one who did. This is how I arrived at this 7% figure. In my book, *Defending the King James Bible*, page xii, I give a chart with the number of changes which the Westcott and Hort text has made from the Textus Receptus that underlies the King James Bible. The Textus Receptus has 140,521 Greek words. Westcott and Hort has changed these words in the New Testament in 5,604 places. This includes a total of 9,970 Greek words which have been either added, subtracted, or changed in some other way. The Textus Receptus has about 647 pages in the Greek Text or about 217 Greek words per page. The Westcott and Hort changes an average of 15.4 Greek words per page. If you divide 140,521 into 9,970, you get 7.1% of the Greek words that are involved in the differences between the TR and the Westcott and Hort Greek text.

What Does "Preservation" Strictly Mean?

#199 Issue: Samuel Gipp said: "The Lord preserved the Word of God in the King James Bible . . ." (Script, p. 41)

Comment by Dr. Waite This is a confusing statement of Samuel Gipp. In what sense does he mean that *"the Lord preserved the Word of God in the King James Bible"*? If he means preservation of English instead of the preservation of the original Hebrew and Greek words, that is not what preservation means in Psalm 12:6-7. There was no English when the Psalms were written and God promised to preserve His "Words." What "Words" was He talking about? They were the Hebrew/Aramaic and Greek "Words." Many other languages have developed since God promised to preserve His Words in Hebrew and Greek. His Words were not given originally in English. His Words were not given originally in French. His Words were not given originally in Spanish. His Words were not given originally in Italian. His Words were not given originally in Russian. His Words were not given originally in German. His Words **were** given originally in Hebrew and a small amount of Aramaic in the Old Testament and Greek in the New Testament.

When God says He is going to Preserve His Words with a capital "P" strictly speaking He means His Hebrew and Greek Words. Those are the Words that have properly formed the basis of our King James Bible. God's Preserved Hebrew and Greek Words are not the basis for the new versions. The new versions have taken some other basis for their Old Testament and their New Testament. They are not based upon the proper Hebrew and Greek texts. Since the King James Bible is taken from the proper Hebrew and the proper Greek texts; since their translators are so superior; since their technique of translation was so superior; and since their theology is accurate, I believe that the King James Bible "preserves" (with a small "p") by means of accurate translation into the English language, every word of the Hebrew and Greek texts that underlie it.

The Heresies in Egypt in the 2nd Century

#200 Issue: John Ankerberg asked if "information that was preached to the people in Egypt was still good stuff?" (Script, p. 42)

Comment by Dr. Waite: John Ankerberg is referring to manuscripts B and ℵ which were copied and corrupted by heretical Egyptian scribes. The *"information that was preached to the people in Egypt"* was **not** good "stuff." There were no New Testament original Greek manuscripts in Egypt with which to compare these false copies. There were also many heretics in Egypt. Even Dr. Bruce Metzger admits this. He wrote:

> *"Almost **every deviant Christian sect** was represented in Egypt during the second century. Clement* [of Alexandria] *mentions the Valentinians, the Basilidians, the Marcionites, the Peratae, the Encratites, the Docetists, the Haimetites, the Cainites, the Ophites, the Simonians, and the Eutychites. What proportion of Christians in Egypt during the second century were **orthodox** is not known."* [Dr. Bruce Metzger, *Early Versions*, p. 101, as quoted in Dr. Jack Moorman's book, *Early Manuscripts*, p. 40]

#201 Issue: Dan Wallace said: "Then the *Alexandrian Text* was preserved." (Script, p. 42)

Comment by Dr. Waite: These texts were "preserved," but I don't believe it was by God. They were "preserved" by man. This "preservation" was due to two factors: (1) the warm climate of Egypt and (2) their disuse by Christians because of their known errors. So far as I am concerned, this text should NOT have been preserved by anyone, because it is so corrupt.

The Septuagint (LXX) Again

#202 Issue: James White said that Samuel Gipp didn't believe the Septuagint existed B.C. (Script, p. 42)

Comment by Dr. Waite: Try as you will, you cannot find the **entire** Old Testament in Greek before the A.D. format of the fifth column of Origin. You will find only very small portions of the Old Testament in Greek B.C. Even the fictitious and legendary *Letter of Aristeas* mentioned that only the first five books of the Old Testament were translated from Hebrew to Greek--not the entire Old Testament.

The "Alexandrian Manuscripts"

#203 Issue: James White asked when the Alexandrian manuscripts were first called by that name. (Script, p. 43)

Comment by Dr. Waite: Manuscript B, (the Vatican) originated in

Egypt. א (Sinai) is also from the Sinai Peninsula. Since both of these manuscripts are from the Alexandria Egypt area in point of origin, they were called "Alexandrian." Westcott and Hort, in the 1880's referred to them in this way.

#204 Issue: Dan Wallace said: "We don't know where the Alexandrian [family] came from." (Script, p. 43)

Comment by Dr. Waite: How does he know where it came from? We certainly believe that the Westcott and Hort type of text originated in Egypt. They are the ones who named B and א "Alexandrian" and therefore from Egypt.

#205 Issue: Dan Wallace said: "We do not know where Vaticanus came from. We do not know where Sinaiticus came from." (Script, p. 43)

Comment by Dr. Waite: They did come from Egypt. They were found there, and originated there. The Sinai Peninsula is in the Egyptian area. This is where א (the Sinai manuscript) was found. B (the Vatican manuscript) was copied, doctored, and corrected in Egypt. This has generally been agreed to by all parties to this dispute. It is strange that Dan Wallace and others are at this point, for some strange and unknown reason, attempting to distance themselves from the Egyptian origin.

Luke 2:22--Christ a Sinner?

#206 Issue: James White brought up Luke 2:22 and asked about "her purification" and its effect on the Deity of Christ. (Script, p. 43)

Comment by Dr. Waite: The reading here does have a bearing on the Deity of Christ. In Luke 2:22 the NIV reads, "**their** purification" meaning the Lord Jesus Christ along with Mary and Joseph all needed to be purified. It is translated "**her** purification" in the King James Bible. Mary is the only one in need of purification in order to fulfil the Law of Moses stated in Leviticus 12:2-6. Jesus was separate from sin. He was perfect and had no need for purification.

#207 Issue: James White gave some other opinions on Luke 2:22. (Script, p. 44)

Comment by Dr. Waite: An entire speech was given at the Dean Burgon Society meeting in Franklin, Massachusetts in 1995. Pastor Denis Gibson from Toronto, Canada, gave an excellent message on Luke 2:22. You should get this message from the **B.F.T.** It is in the 1995 *Dean Burgon Society Message Book*. All 25 messages are in this book. It is **B.F.T. #2565-P**, 247 pages @ **$25.00 + P&H.**

#208 Issue: James White continued talking about Luke 2:22 and his alleged documentation. (Script, p. 44)

Comment by Dr. Waite: Dr. Jack Moorman wrote *Early*

Manuscripts and the Authorized Version a Closer Look--with Manuscript Evidence and Summary, (It is **B.F.T. #1825**, 157 pages @ **$15.00** + **P&H**). On page 86, Dr. Moorman gives the analysis of where the "**her** purification" comes from. It is in the cursives: pc, the Old Latin: l and r1, (a, aur, b, beta, c, d, e, ff2, l, r1, and the Vulgate. Just because B and ℵ (the Vatican and Sinai) have "**their** purification," that does not mean that this is the correct translation.

#209 Issue: James White said: "Even Erasmus desired to use Vaticanus. (Script, p. 44)

Comment by Dr. Waite: That is false and misleading! Erasmus did not desire to "use" Vaticanus in the sense that he accepted its false readings and wished to adopt them as his own. He sought various readings from it to compare with the true Textus Receptus readings. He purposely rejected the readings of the Vatican manuscript B and its allies.

Alexandrian Text Never the "Majority"

#210 Issue: Dan Wallace said of the Alexandrian text that: "It was in the majority for the first nine centuries." (Script, p. 44)

Comment by Dr. Waite: This is absolutely false! Let's look at Dan Wallace's chart that is page 45 of the script. It's called the "Distribution of Greek MSS by Century and Text Type." In the first place, let me remind you that, as Dean Burgon has argued convincingly, there is no such thing as a "text type" except in the mind of Westcott and Hort and their followers. This term implies genealogical relationships between the manuscripts which are not present. There are not "text types," there are merely Greek manuscripts.

Remember the maxim: "Figures don't lie, but liars can figure." Dan Wallace's chart is a lying chart. Just because it is simple and clear does not make it true! On Dan Wallace's chart he has three alleged "text types": Alexandrian, Western, and Byzantine, all of which are figments of his own imagination. Where is the fourth alleged "text type," the Caesarean? He has the Byzantine text not even appearing on the scene until the 5th century. If he means by this the Textus Receptus, this was the text of the original Greek New Testament! Dan Wallace used in 1995 the same argument that Westcott and Hort used back in 1881.

Dean John William Burgon proved this to be false in the 1870's and 1880's. He amassed an index of over 86,000 quotations or allusions to the New Testament from the writings of 76 early Church Fathers. This index with these quotations is still in the British Museum in London, England. Edward Miller, who edited Dean Burgon's book after his death, completed *The Traditional Text of the Holy Gospels*. Burgon and Miller produced statistics on Bible quotations or allusions from 76 early Church Fathers. These quotations prove that Dan Wallace's chart is false. Here Dan Wallace is denying that there was a Textus Receptus or Traditional Text before the 5th Century. What he is saying is that the Alexandrian text was in the majority for the first nine centuries.

What about the research and proof of Dean Burgon? In this book on pages 99-101, he lists the 76 Church Fathers plus the numbers of quotations or allusions to the Bible of two different types (the Neologian [Westcott/Hort B/א type] and the Traditional type). All of these Church Father's died in 400 A.D. or before, but many of them were from the 2nd, 3rd, and 4th centuries! This certainly is within the 5th century! In this evidence, the Traditional Text was present in a majority of **3 to 2** over the Westcott/Hort/B/א type of text. That's a 60% to 40% ratio in favor of the Traditional Text that underlies the King James Bible.

Dr. Jack Moorman has even found more early Church Father's quotations than this. His more recent study found the percentage to be 70% to 30% in favor of the Traditional Text over the B/א type of texts!

The History of B and א

#211 Issue: Dr. Chambers said: "That's not the question I asked."
(Script, p. 44)

Comment by Dr. Waite: That's exactly right. The question he asked was how do you account for the fact that, at an early date, the churches rejected the Westcott and Hort type of text of B and A and did not start using it again until 1881 when Westcott and Hort made their new Greek Text based upon the B and A 4th century manuscripts. In reality, for 1500 years (from 381 A.D. to 1881 A.D.) the churches used a different Greek text of the New Testament. That was Dr. Chamber's question.

#212 Issue: Dr. Chambers gave the history of the B and א, the Westcott and Hort type of text. He said, in part: "Only in 1881 when Westcott and Hort brought it back . . ." (Script, p. 44)

Comment by Dr. Waite: Dr. Chambers said it right again. Do you believe that God would take away His true Words for 1500 years from the churches? I do not believe that. I believe that the early churches knew better than Dan Wallace and John Ankerberg what was and what was not the proper Greek text of the New Testament. The early church saw the corruptions of B and the corruptions of A and the corruptions of the others that went along with B and A. They laid these corrupted manuscripts aside, put them out of their minds, and continued to copy from the original words that were given by Paul and John and the other New Testament writers. Those words have come down to us, and I believe we have them, in the Textus Receptus which underlies the King James Bible. These new versions have gone all the way back to the 4th century corruptions of B and A to take their Greek text. This is the wrong Greek text.

#213 Issue: Dan Wallace said: "Obviously not all the words of Jesus are written down." (Script, p. 44)

Comment by Dr. Waite: God gave us in His Bible only what He deemed necessary for us in this age and the ages to come.

Doctrine of Bible Preservation Denied

#214 Issue: Dan Wallace said: "Your doctrine of preservation is based on a faulty exegesis of a handful of passages that you extrapolate. . . . And then you say, 'This refers just to the *King James'* without any shred of evidence whatsoever, except your own reason." (Script, p. 46)

Comment by Dr. Waite: Dan Wallace denies God's promise to preserve the very WORDS of the Hebrew and Greek originals. This is serious error. It is also an error in his remark about the King James Bible. I myself do **not** say that Preservation, such as mentioned in Psalm 12:6-7, refers to the English of the King James Bible. This promise has nothing to do with the English King James Bible. English was not even invented when this Psalm was written. The Preservation that God promises for His Words has to do with the Old Testament Hebrew and, by analogy, the New Testament Greek manuscripts. The reason I say that the King James Bible is "God's Word kept in tact in English" is because that is the only Bible that takes the proper Hebrew and Greek words which have been Preserved and puts them accurately into English. The primary Preservation promised is **not** in the English Bible, it is not in the German Bible, it is not in the French Bible, it is not in the Spanish Bible, it is only in the original manuscripts of Hebrew, Aramaic, and Greek. From God's Preserved manuscripts of Hebrew, Aramaic, and Greek we are to translate accurately the Bible into all the languages of the world.

#215 Issue: Dr. Chambers asked "what birthed the Reformation?" (Script, p. 46)

Comment by Dr. Waite: Of course the answer is the Traditional Text which underlies our King James Bible and the Bibles of that time.

#216 Issue: Dan Wallace made the comment about how God works "through the remnant." (Script, p. 46)

Comment by Dr. Waite: In the case of the New Testament Greek manuscripts, the remnant is the Westcott and Hort (B and ℵ) Geek text. This is the text which has less than 1% of the evidence. The remnant is not how God works concerning the preservation of His Word. Many times God does work through the minority of people that are right, but when He is preserving His Words He has preserved 99% of the manuscripts for us in the kind of Greek text that underlies our King James Bible's New Testament.

Changes in the Nestle-Aland Text

#217 Issue: Don Wilkins commented on whether or not the Nestle-

Aland text changed any of its latest text to conform to the Textus Receptus. He thought they went back to the Western Text instead. (Script, p. 47)

Comment by Dr. Waite: I don't know about that statement. I haven't checked this out. That was not my quotation; it was Mrs. Riplinger's quote. I am sure she has evidence to corroborate it in her book on *New Age Bible Versions*.

#218 Issue: James White said to Dr. Chambers: "You're demonstrating that there is no conspiracy." (Script, p. 47)

Comment by Dr. Waite: Who's talking about a conspiracy? No one mentioned this term. Why does James White bring it up? James White is trying to argue against Mrs. Riplinger's *New Age Bible Versions*. He is trying to make Dr. Chambers fit in with her book and viewpoint. James White is not talking to Mrs. Riplinger, he is talking to Dr. Chambers. Mrs. Riplinger purposely did not want to be on this telecast because she knew that they would go off on some little wild rabbit trail tangent. As you can see; that is what they have done.

"Mixed Texts"

#219 Issue: Dan Wallace talked about "mixed texts." (Script, p. 47)

Comment by Dr. Waite: The mixed texts, whenever they had Textus Receptus readings and other readings together, instead of calling it a Textus Receptus text, they call it another text (either the Alexandrian, Western, Caesarean, or whatever). That is a serious flaw in their argument. When you have a Textus Receptus reading mixed in here with these other readings of the, so-called, Alexandrian or B and ℵ type of reading, which text is it? We would call it a Textus Receptus text. They would call it the Alexandrian text. If the Textus Receptus is there it ought to be a testimony in favor of the Textus Receptus.

A False "General Edited Text"

#220 Issue: Dan Wallace talked about a "general edited text." (Script, p. 47)

Comment by Dr. Waite: By his use of the term, "general edited text," Dan Wallace made reference to the so-called "recension theory." This theory is just that--"theory." It has no basis in history or in fact. The Textus Receptus is not a "general edited text." If any text is a "general edited text," it is that of B and ℵ which was the basis of the Westcott and Hort Greek text. The Textus Receptus is simply copies of copies which had their origin in the New Testament autographs themselves. This is a repetition of the false argument of Westcott and Hort found in their *Introduction to the Greek Text*. The false argument alleges that in 250 A.D. and then again in 350 A.D. there was a recension or an edited text of the Greek New Testament. In this so-called recension or edition, all of the B and ℵ type of manuscripts were discarded. The only ones that were kept were those that conformed to what we know as the Textus Receptus or the Received Text. This was the only way that Westcott and Hort could account for the fact that their idols (B and ℵ) formed less than 1% of the Greek manuscripts that survived the centuries and the Textus Receptus manuscripts formed over 99% of the Greek Manuscripts.

That is a faulty argument since there is no historical proof of any kind that there was any such editorship, addition, and recension made of the Greek Text. Certainly such a momentous event would have found some mention either in secular or sacred historical records had it taken place. There is not one single mention of this event, hence it did not take place. It was merely a **theory** of Westcott and Hort without any basis in fact.

A False "Recension" Theory

#221 Issue: Dan Wallace continued to explain this false recension theory. He said that the alleged "editors" of the Textus Receptus thought: "It's better to include things that aren't there than it is to lose something that might originally be there." (Script, p. 47)

Comment by Dr. Waite: Dean Burgon is very clear against the concept of a "recension" of the Traditional Text. Let me quote from his book, *The Revision Revised* (**B.F.T. #611**, 640 pages in hardback @ **$25.00 + P&H**). On pages 272-273, Burgon quoted from Westcott and Hort's own *Introduction of the Greek New Testament*. This is available as **B.F.T. #1303**, 530 pages, @ **$15.00 +P&H**. Westcott and Hort are quoted as saying:

> *'The Syrian Text* [which is our Textus Receptus] *must be in fact the result of a 'Recension,'* . . . *performed deliberately by Editors, and not merely by Scribes.--{Ibid.)"*

That is the false theory that Dan Wallace is trying to perpetrate here when he says that the Textus Receptus or Traditional Text is a "general edited text." Here is Dean Burgon's answer to the false statement of Westcott and Hort:

> *"But why `must' it? Instead of 'must--in fact,' we are disposed to read 'may--in fiction.' The learned Critic can but mean that, on comparing the text of Fathers of the IVth century with the Text of cod. B, it becomes to himself self-evident that one of the two has been fabricated. Granted. Then--why should not the solitary Codex be the offending party? For what imaginable reason should cod. B--which comes to us without a character, and which, when tried by the test of primitive Antiquity, stands convicted of 'univera vitiositas,' (to use Tischendorf's expression);-- why (we ask) should codex B be upheld `contra mundum' ?"*

On pages 293-294, Burgon again wrote:

> *"Apart however from the gross intrinsic improbability of the supposed Recension,--the utter absence of one particle of evidence, traditional or otherwise, that it ever did take place, must be held to be fatal to the*

hypothesis that it did. It is simply incredible that an incident of such magnitude and interest would leave no trace of itself in history. As a conjecture--(and it only professes to be conjecture)--Dr. Hort's notion of how the Text of the Fathers of the IIIrd, IVth, and Vth centuries,-- which, as he truly remarks is in the main identical with our own Received Text,--came into being, must be unconditionally abandoned."

This is a very important quotation. Dr. Hort says the Textus Receptus is a recension and that the editors got together to change it. There is no evidence for this whatsoever. On page 294 Dean Burgon again says:

"We have been so full on the subject of this imaginary 'Antiochian' or 'Syrian text,' not (the reader may be sure) without sufficient reason. Scant satisfaction truly is there in scattering to the winds an airy tissue which its ingenious authors have been industriously weaving __for 30 years__.But it is clear that with this hypothesis of a 'Syrian' text,-- the immediate source and actual prototype of the commonly received Text of the N.T.,--stands or falls their entire Textual theory. Reject it, and the entire fabric is observed to collapse, and subside into a shapeless ruin. And with it, of necessity, goes the 'New Greek Text,'-- and therefore the 'New English Version' of our Revisionists, which in the main has been founded on it."

If you knock out the theory that there was an edited recension in 250 A.D. and 350 A.D., you knock out the New Greek text that they have concocted based upon that theory. If you knock out the New Greek Text, you also knock out the "New English Version" that is based upon it. If you knock out this English Revised Version of 1881, you knock out every other English version that is based upon virtually that same false Greek text namely: The New International Version, the New American Standard Version, the Living Version, and all the other modern versions of our day. On page 296-297 Den Burgon again says:

"Drs. Westcott and Hort assume that this 'Antiochian text'--found in the later cursives and the Fathers of the latter half of the IVth century--must be an artificial, an arbitrarily invented standard; a text fabricated between A.D. 250 and A.D. 350. And if they may but be so fortunate as to persuade the world to adopt their hypothesis, then all will be easy; for they will have reduced the supposed `consent of Fathers' to the reproduction of one and the same single `primary documentary witness:' . . . Upset the hypothesis on the other hand, and all is reversed in a moment. Every attesting Father is perceived to be a dated MS. and an independent authority; and the combined evidence of several of these becomes simply unmanageable. In like manner, `the approximate consent of the cursives,' . . . is perceived to be equivalent not to 'A Primary Documentary Witness,'--not to 'ONE

Antiochian Original,'--but to be tantamount to the articulate speech of many witnesses of high character, coming to us from every quarter of primitive Christendom. "

You can see the importance of pointing out Dan Wallace's false statement here concerning what he called a "general edited text."

#222 Issue: James White asked unbelievingly regarding the preservation of the text of Scripture: "Did He do so by, for example, having one religious group in one religious area grab hold of the text and hold the originals or something like that?" (Script, p. 47)

Comment by Dr. Waite: Well, yes , this is exactly what God did! God sent the original New Testament Greek manuscripts to the original areas which were the recipients of the books such as Ephesus, Colosse, or Phillipi. This was the group that held the originals and copies were made from them.

James White Denies Bible Corruption

#223 Issue: In speaking of the doctrinal corruption of the Bible, James White said: "It was not within the capacity of man to corrupt the Scriptures in that way." (Script, p. 48)

Comment by Dr. Waite: This is another false statement! James White certainly has an erroneous view of the nature of man. I believe in the depravity of man! Depraved, unregenerate man has every "capacity" in him "to corrupt the Scriptures." We have already listed a number of heretics that have corrupted the Scriptures in a doctrinal manner. These heretics are spoken of in church history.

#224 Issue: John Ankerberg, talking about "mistakes" in the New Testament Greek text, said: "They're not all going to make the same mistake in the same spot." (Script, p. 48)

Comment by Dr. Waite: They're trying to convey to the listeners that there is variation and even mistakes, corruptions, and changes in the New Testament Greek text. This is not the thing that ought to be stressed. If you want to talk about B and ℵ (the Vatican and Sinai, the false Alexandrian texts, the Westcott and Hort texts) you have thousands of variations, corruptions and "mistakes." If you are talking about the Textus Receptus type of text or the Traditional Text or the Byzantine Text, those manuscripts are remarkable in that they are almost identical and the variations are so few. Many variations involve only the spelling of names and other minor things. That's the remarkable thing about the over 99% (5,510) of the manuscripts that go along with our King James Bible and its Textus Receptus.

We should not be commenting on variations, mistakes, or differences. We should be stressing the fact of the similarities. Because the Textus Receptus Text manuscripts which underlie our King James Bible are so similar, Westcott and Hort were very upset and troubled. They had to explain how these texts were so similar and practically identical. That is why they had to concoct this false theory of the recensions or editions of 250 A.D. and 350 A.D. They had to give their false explanation of why these manuscripts were almost identical. Didn't James White say on page 48 of the Script, near **"Comment #223"** that it was *"not within the capacity of man to corrupt the Scriptures"*? So how can he believe both that and the recension theory which alleges that men did corrupt the Scriptures? I was just wondering. Is this not "circular reasoning"?

An Erroneous Illustration

#225 Issue: John Ankerberg used an illustration about "A" students and B students copying things. (Script, p. 48)

Comment by Dr. Waite: John Ankerberg used an unfortunate illustration of two kinds of students ("A" students and "B" students) who copied the same material. The "A" students, according to the analogy of John Ankerberg, are similar to those copying B and א. He considered these to be the good copiers. These he likened to the manuscripts which Westcott and Hort and their followers used. In reality these manuscripts are the worst that have ever seen the light of day.

#226 Issue: Dan Wallace, in this analogy of students' copying material, implies that errors were made in the New Testament. (Script, p. 48)

Comment by Dr. Waite: Dan Wallace tells his students to purposely change what they were copying for theological reasons or eliminate a few words or some other thing. He seems to be trying to prove that these men who are copying the scriptures were leaving out words?

Many Manuscripts Not Being Used

#227 Issue: John Ankerberg, speaking of God, said: "He didn't just give us one document that came down that we can all worship. He has given us thousands . . ." (Script, p. 48)

Comment by Dr. Waite: If that's the case, why do these people practically worship the **"one"** manuscript B (Vatican). This **is** what they are doing. They are worshiping **one** manuscript. In their *Introduction to the Greek New Testament*, Westcott and Hort's argument is summed up as follows.

B is the manuscript that Westcott and Hort have forced upon the unbelieving and the believing world. Westcott and Hort said that B is the most neutral of all other manuscripts and no matter what other manuscripts say, if you can get א (Sinai) to agree with B they believe that is the original wording. If א doesn't agree with B, then get another major manuscript that agrees with B (Vatican). Then the two of them that agree together becomes, for Westcott and Hort and their followers, the original wording of the New Testament text. Westcott and Hort maintain, in their *Introduction to the Greek New Testament* of 1881, if you cannot get a single solitary manuscript to agree with B (the Vatican) then take B and B alone. Now, when John Ankerberg says, God has not just given us one document, my friend, the text that underlies our King James Bible, the Textus Receptus is not simply one document. The power of God's preservation of His Words is **not** that we only have one document, but that we have thousands (5,210) of documents and basically they all agree. This agreement proves that these approximately 45 manuscripts of Westcott and Hort and B and ℵ are false.

#228 Issue: John Ankerberg said of the manuscripts we now have: "by looking at <u>all</u> of these and comparing them, they didn't all make the mistakes in the same spot." (Script, p. 48)

Comment by Dr. Waite: Notice John Ankerberg said: "By looking at <u>all</u> of these and comparing them." "**All** of these" includes, as of 1967 by Kurt Aland's own count, 5,255 Greek Manuscripts that have preserved for us today. Do you know how many manuscripts that the Westcott and Hort believers of today look at? They only look at 45 manuscripts in all, or less than 1% of the evidence! That is B and ℵ and 43 other manuscripts. They do **not** examine the other 5,210 manuscripts, or more than 99% of the evidence! In fact they do not even collate them. All they are doing is saying that B and ℵ are correct and when these two false manuscripts say something they wrongly believe them to be correct.

#229 Issue: Dr. Chambers mentioned that the Alexandrian text has only about 40 or 50 manuscripts. (Script, p. 49)

Comment by Dr. Waite: Dr. Chambers has got it right on target! According to Dr. Jack Moorman's book, *Forever Settled* (**B.F.T. #1428**, 217 large pages, @ **$21.00** +P&H), there are only about 45 manuscripts out of the 5,255 plus that we have. This is less than 1% of the evidence. Dr. Chambers is exactly right.

#230 Issue: Dr. Chambers said, "I question . . ." and then was interrupted. (Script, p. 49)

Comment by Dr. Waite: At this point, they didn't let Dr. Chambers speak. They cut him off and ran right over his thought.

False Statements About Church Fathers

#231 Issue: John Ankerberg quoted Josh McDowell's book and said that if you did away with all the New Testament manuscripts, "you could replace the entire New Testament by just looking at the Church Fathers and how they quoted the New Testament except for 8 verses." (Script, p. 49)

Comment by Dr. Waite: I don't believe that at all! I don't believe that the Church Fathers can give us all of the New Testament. The Church Fathers did quote some portions of the New Testament that's correct. Dean Burgon has amassed over 86,000 quotations of or allusions to the New Testament from the Church Fathers. He has analyzed them and found a ratio of 3 to 2 in favor of Textus Receptus quotes. This is 1.5 to 1 or 60% to 40%. If indeed the early Church Fathers are looked at Dr. Jack Moorman found recently even a higher ratio, that is a 2.3 to 1 ratio or 70% to 30% of Textus Receptus quotations or allusions versus B an ℵ readings. This is found in **B.F.T. #2136**, 63 large pages @ **$6.00 + P&H** which is available from the Bible for Today. Both Dean Burgon and Dr. Moorman examined only the Church Fathers who died 400 A.D. or before. It is highly improbable that their quotations can come up with all the New Testament except eight verses.

#232 Issue: Arthur Farstad said: **"That is true that you can reconstruct a New Testament." (Script, p. 49)**

Comment by Dr. Waite: Again, I don't agree that you can reconstruct a New Testament from Church Fathers' quotations or allusions. Even Arthur Farstad admitted that the Church Fathers quoted often from memory and were not exact. What sort of a text would that be? Though this is true, you can at least tell which text they were quoting from, whether from the Textus Receptus or from the B and ℵ errors.

#233 Issue: John Ankerberg said this was **"more information to compare in terms of getting back to what the Apostles actually wrote." (Script, p. 49)**

Comment by Dr. Waite: That's true. But from these early Church Fathers' quotations or allusions, the Textus Receptus type of text is seen to have been used in a ratio of either 60% to 40 % (Dean Burgon's figures) or 70% to 30% (Dr. Jack Moorman's figures). These truths are not accepted by John Ankerberg and his companions.

The Confusing NKJV Footnotes

#234 Issue: Arthur Farstad said: **"We shouldn't be criticized for having notes in the *New King James* that show critical and *Majority Text* readings." (Script, p. 49)**

Comment by Dr. Waite: Arthur Farstad is justifying the NKJV textual footnotes in their study edition. The notes in the New King James Version of the Scripture of the New Testament are destructive and confusing, in my judgment. Satan is happy with these because he is the "author of confusion" (1 Corinthians 14:33). These notes are an admission that they really don't know which readings are correct and which are in error. At the top of the page, the NKJV claims to be translating from the Textus Receptus. In the notes, however, they give the readings from the "NU" (Nestle-Aland/United Bible Societies Texts). This is the old Westcott and Hort type of text. In addition to the "NU," they have the "MT" ("Majority Text") readings. In my book, *Defending the King James Bible*, I have criticized the New King James Version for doing this. This casts doubt. When you see a note doubting the last twelve verses of Mark you don't know which is right. God is not the "author of confusion" (1 Corinthians 14:33). In the New International Version and The New American Standard Version you don't see any footnotes showing another reading. They only have their own reading. Why, in the New King James, do they waffle in their opinion. In fact, in the back part of the study edition, they boast about having the reader being able to be a textual critic for himself and to leave out portions that he doesn't think should be there.

> **#235 Issue:** John Ankerberg, commenting on the New King James footnotes, said: "which is nothing more than they did in the 1611 edition." (Script, p. 49)

Comment by Dr. Waite: This is absolutely false! They didn't do that in the 1611 edition at all. They never put in what the Westcott and Hort readings were and what the Majority Text reading was throughout the New Testament! That is as false as the day is long. Either John Ankerberg doesn't know what the 1611 edition is, or if he does know what it is, he is falsely stating his case. If you want a printed edition put out by Nelson (we carry it in the Bible for Today, it is **B.F.T. #1102 @ $32.00 + P&H**) you can see that the notes in the 1611 King James Edition have **very little** to do with variant readings.

A False View of Greek Manuscripts

> **#236 Issue:** Dr. Chambers, quoting from an NIV book, said: "The NIV says basically in this book that they used Vaticanus and Sinaiticus." (Script, p. 49)

Comment by Dr. Waite: That is true! The NIV basically **does** go by the Vaticanus and Sinaiticus (B and ℵ).

> **#237 Issue:** Dan Wallace refers to his chart called "The Myth about Modern Translations" which is Chart #2, on page 50 of the script. (Script, p. 49)

Comment by Dr. Waite: If you look at Chart No. 2 on page 50 you see that Dan Wallace says it is a myth that the King James Bible goes back to the 2nd century. Actually, the text which underlies it goes back to the 1st century. If you look at Dan Wallace's Chart No. 3 on page 51 which is called "The Manuscripts Behind the Modern Translations" he is trying to correct this, so-called myth. The chart alleges that the number of manuscripts which underlie the king James Bible are only "six" and he dates them from the 12th century. That is the myth! The manuscripts which underlie our King James Bible are many more than six! There are over 5,210 manuscripts that underlie the Textus Receptus used by the King James Bible. The **Greek words** which are behind the King James Bible go back to the first century originals, regardless of the date of the copies! This chart alleges that the NIV has 5,000 manuscripts behind it. The question I have is out of those 5,000 manuscripts how many did they use? They used B and ℵ and perhaps 43 others--a total of only 45 out of the 5,255 manuscripts available as of 1967. This is less than 1% of the evidence. This is a false and a lying chart!

#238 Issue: Dan Wallace said that the King James Bible was based "essentially on six manuscripts that Erasmus used that came from about the tenth to the thirteenth century, most of them from the twelfth century." (Script, p. 49)

Comment by Dr. Waite: The King James Bible is **not** based on the Erasmus Greek text. It is based on Beza's 5th edition text of 1598. I don't believe that the figure of "six manuscripts" is true, either. I believe there were a few others. Erasmus searched the libraries of Europe comparing Greek manuscripts. He used the manuscripts he felt were most faithful. The **materials** on which the **words** were written might be from later centuries, but it is most important to see that the **words** were copied from the first century originals.

#239 Issue: Dan Wallace said: "The revised version of 1881 was based on 2,000 manuscripts." (Script, p. 49)

Comment by Dr. Waite: This revised version of 1881 was based primarily on B and ℵ. They may have had 2,000 manuscripts at the time, but they didn't use them. If you look at the *Introduction of the Greek Text* written by Hort, you will find that they based the ERV of 1881 on B (the Vatican Manuscript), on ℵ (the Sinai Manuscript), and on manuscripts that agreed with them.

#240 Issue: Dan Wallace said, speaking of the NIV: "Now we're basing it on over 5,000 manuscripts." (Script, p. 52)

Comment by Dr. Waite: They have **not** based the New International Version on 5,000 manuscripts. It is true that we have 5,255 manuscripts as of 1967, and there are about 100 more since then. They didn't use these 5,255 manuscripts. They used B, ℵ, and those approximately 43 others that agreed with them. You may have 1,000 books in your library, but if you don't use them, does that mean that you base all of your statements on those 1,000 books? No, you base your statements on the one or two that you use. You don't base them on the entire 1000 books.

#241 Issue: Dan Wallace defended his 2,000 and 5,000 numbers of manuscripts respectively that formed the basis of the ERV of 1881 and the NIV of 1973. (Script, p. 52)

Comment by Dr. Waite: The number of manuscripts is absolutely false! The manuscripts used for the 1881 version was not 2,000. The number of manuscripts which is claimed to be used in the NIV is false as well. In both instances there is only one principle manuscript which is used and that is the Vatican manuscript, B. B is worshiped and used more than any other manuscript. Where changes occurred in the Textus Receptus they occurred because B and/or its allies said so. That is why they changed the text. The versions today (NIV, NASV, RSV, and the footnotes of the NKJV) are basically based on one manuscript and that is B.

#242 Issue: Dan Wallace said: "The King James was based on Erasmus' text of six manuscripts, and he looked at a little bit more material." (Script, p. 52)

Comment by Dr. Waite: Here is this lie again. The King James Bible is not based on 6 manuscripts of Erasmus. It was based upon Beza's 5th edition Greek text of 1558. If, in fact, only 6 manuscripts were used they were six very accurate and representative manuscripts; because now we have 5,210 manuscripts which are almost identical to his. The text which underlies our King James Bible rests upon an average of 99% of all the manuscripts. This includes the uncials, the papyri, the cursives, and the Lectionaries. The King James Bible has a wide base, much wider than any other English version in existence. Dan Wallace is trying to imply that the King James Bible has a slim, narrow, thin base of six manuscripts. This is entirely false. To say that the Westcott and Hort text of 1881 was based on 2,000 manuscripts is simply a fairy tale. To say that the NIV is based on 5,000 manuscripts is also a fantasy. Dan Wallace is a falsifier of truth.

#243 Issue: Arthur Farstad said that the King James Bible was based on "the *Complutensian Polyglot* and *Beza*." (Script, p. 52)

Comment by Dr. Waite: Dan Wallace was wrong saying that the basis of the King James Bible was the Greek text of Erasmus. Arthur Farstad was half wrong by including the *Complutensian Polyglot* as its basis. It was Beza's 5th edition, 1598, which was the exact text on which the King James Bible was based. It was certainly not the Erasmus text. If you want to see a scholarly work of the exact Greek Text on which the King James Bible was based, you may request from us the original Greek Text of Dr. F.H.A. Scrivener. This is **B.F.T. #1670**, 668 pages @ **$35.00 + P&H.** You will not find it based on the Erasmus text, but on the Beza text with only 190 exceptions that didn't follow that particular edition. Dr. K. D. DiVietro found even fewer than 190 exceptions. In fact, he did not find any, after checking carefully.

#244 Issue: When Arthur Farstad said "Beza, mostly Beza," correcting himself properly, Dan Wallace said: "I'm not so sure it was mostly Beza." (Script, p. 52)

Comment by Dr. Waite: Dan Wallace is in serious error here, as in many other places. He is just plain wrong here and refuses to admit that he doesn't know something. He needs to write us for Dr. F.H.A. Scriveners original Greek text and see that it was based firmly on Beza's 5th edition of 1598. Dr. F.H.A. Scrivener was on the English Revised Committee of 1881. He was one of the greatest Greek scholars of his day. He proclaims that this Greek text is Beza's text of 1598. This is the text that the King James Bible is based on with about 190 places where the translators chose another source. The sources consulted by Dr. Scrivener, according to his APPENDIX, page 648, are listed as:

> *"[1] Complutensian Polyglot N.T., 1514; [2] Erasmus' (1516, 1519, 1522, 1527, 1535); [3] Aldus' 1518; [4] Colinaeus' 1534; [5] Stephanus' (1546, 1549, 1550, 1551); [6] Plantin (Antwerp Polyglott) 1572; [7] Beza's (1560, 1565, 1582, 1589, 1598); [8] Vulgate Latin; [9] Tyndale's English 1526; [10] Authorised Version 1611."* [Dr. Frederick H. A. Scrivener, *The New Testament in Greek According to the Text Followed in the Authorised Version Together with the Variations Adopted in the Revised Version*, 1881, p. 648]

This is in Dr. Scrivener's scholarly and thorough APPENDIX with the exact Greek changes listed. The changes are listed in his work cited above, pages 648-656. The book is available in reprint form as **B.F.T. #1670**, 668 pages @ **$35.00 + P&H**.

False Early Church Fathers Information

> **#245 Issue:** Dan Wallace quoted Kurt Aland to the effect that up until the time of Asterius, who died in 341 A.D., "no Church Father used the *Byzantine Text* as a text." (Script, p. 52)

Comment by Dr. Waite: Dan Wallace's point of "as a text" is extremely subjective. I maintain that if a Church Father quoted or alluded to a word or verse that was unique to the Textus Receptus, Traditional Text, then obviously he had that TEXT in his hand. I have mentioned before the excellent book, *Early Church Fathers and the Authorized Version a Demonstration*, by Dr. Jack Moorman. This is a companion volume to, *Early Manuscripts and The Authorized Version*, On pages 34 and 35 of *Early Church Fathers* he gives a list of the Church Fathers and their quotations from the Textus Receptus type of manuscripts or the, so-called, Byzantine text. This is **B.F.T. #2136**, 63 pages, @ **$6.00 + P&H**. To have Kurt Aland state this falsehood and to have Dan Wallace perpetuate it is unfortunate.

It is FALSE to state that no Church Father prior to Asterius, who died in the year A.D. 341, used the Byzantine or Received type of Greek text. As mentioned in *Early Church Fathers and the Authorized Version*, pages 34-45, Dr. Moorman found the following: Ignatius who lived in 110 A.D. quoted from the Textus Receptus type of text three different times. Polycarp who died in 156 A.D. quoted from the Textus Receptus four times. Tatian who wrote in 170 A.D. quoted from the Textus Receptus sixty-six times. Irenaeus died in the year 202 A.D. quoted from the Textus Receptus fifteen times. Tertullian died in 220 A.D. and quoted from the Textus Receptus thirty-six times. Hippolytus died in 235 A.D. and quoted from the Textus Receptus six times. For all 40 of these early Church Fathers and other early documents, see Dr. Moorman's work. It is **B.F.T. #2136**, 63 pages, @ **$6.00 + P&H**. The above early Church Fathers and many more will disprove Dan Wallace's assertion. It is not true to make a distinction between a Textus Receptus "reading" and a Textus Receptus "text." To have a READING, the writer must have also had the TEXT to go along with it!

#246 Issue: Dan Wallace kept repeating the "Asterius" false argument. (Script, p. 52)

Comment by Dr. Waite: As mentioned above in #245 Issue, Asterius was **not** the first one to quote from the Byzantine/Traditional/Textus Receptus.

#247 Issue: Dan Wallace said that Asterius who he alleges to have first used the Byzantine Text was himself a heretic. He said that this doesn't make the Byzantine Text a heretical text, but the implication is there. (Script p. 51)

Comment by Dr. Waite: He is implying that the Byzantine text is heretical because heretics used it. This is false logic. If heretics quoted from the Textus Receptus, it is because they had it in their hands. This is true of many of the early heretics. We are not accepting their heresies, but are using their quotations of Scripture at the time when they wrote to prove the antiquity of the Received/Traditional/Textus Receptus text. (Script, p. 52)

More on Lesbian Mollenkott and the NIV

#248 Issue: Kenneth Barker denied that Virginia Mollenkott was a "member of the *NIV* translation committee." He said "She was not, she is not, never has been." (Script, p. 53)

Comment by Dr. Waite: In the original advertisement for the New International Version, Virginia Mollenkott was labeled as a "**translator**." Kenneth Barker is not telling the truth at this point. The translators were listed and her name is on the list. I have this advertisement. If you are interested in having it contact the **B.F.T.** and we can prove this to you. This false information was first promulgated by the publishers of the NIV. Why should he be blaming those who read and believed their announcements?

Is the NIV "The Word of God"?

#249 Issue: Kenneth Barker said he could hold his NIV in his hand and say, "This is the Word of God." (Script, p. 53)

Comment by Dr. Waite: I cannot pick up Kenneth Barker's NIV and say that *"this is the Word of God"* when it has a Greek Text which changes the Textus Receptus in over 5,604 places and adds, subtracts or changes in some other way the Greek or Hebrew text in well over 6,653 places. The New International Versions has been besmirched, sullied, dirtied, and filthified by those perverted words of men. The same is true, to a lesser degree, of the New American Standard Version. There are over 4,000 examples that I have found by my own research where they have added, subtracted, or changed in some other way words that are in the proper Hebrew or the Greek texts. In the New King James Version they have in the footnotes these other texts and there are over 2,000 examples of addition, subtraction and changing of the Words of God. I cannot hold up these other versions as Bibles, but I **can** hold up the King James Bible and say, because of its superior texts, translators, technique, and theology that *"This is the Word of God kept in tact in English."*

What Version Should People Use?

#250 Issue: John Ankerberg asked all the participants to tell the audience which version of the Bible they think people should use. (Script, p. 53)

Comment by Dr. Waite: Kenneth Barker didn't do what John Ankerberg asked him to do. He didn't answer the question. The question was to give an answer to *"which English translation of the Bible do you think people should use today?"* "Which" doesn't mean ?how many." Kenneth Barker said to use them all. It would seem that he should have said to use the New International Version. That is the paraphrase he helped to construct.

Still More on Lesbian Mollenkott &NIV

#251 Issue: Dr. Chambers said that Virginia Mollenkott was "listed under the whole group of <u>translators</u> and that's probably how that got listed as a <u>translation committee</u>." (Script, p. 53)

Comment by Dr. Waite: He is correct. Let me just quote from the New International Version's *"<u>Translators</u>, Translation Process, the Reviews, the Choice of Editions."* This is from Zondervan. It has Kenneth Barker's picture on it. It carries a huge headline "**THE TRANSLATORS**." It lists all the names of those whom THEY consider to be a "<u>translator</u>." If they had not wanted to have Virginia Mollenkott listed as a "**TRANSLATOR**," they should have kept her name off that list!! This brochure says:

> *"Although the scores of <u>translators</u> and editors come from different denominations and educational institutions, they hold one conviction in common and that their task is a sacred task to honor the Bible as the inspired Word of God. The following is a partial list of these scholars."*

On this list is Virginia Mollenkott from William Patterson College. Dr. Joseph Chambers is absolutely correct!

Who Is Splitting the Churches?

> **#252 Issue:** James White said, in speaking of people standing for the King James Bible: "Churches are split, ministries are decimated by this type of thing." (Script, p. 54)

Comment by Dr. Waite: If the Bible is of any importance what could be more important than which Bible we use. Before the new versions came out (the New American Standard Version, the New International Version, the New King James Version or any of these other versions) most of us had but one Bible, the King James Bible. Fundamental Christians preached from it, memorized from it, taught from it, believed it, and tried to live it. James White is saying that churches are being spilt and decimated because people are still standing for the King James Bible. No, no, a thousand times, no! The reason for the "split" and "decimation" in some local churches is the emergence and the combativeness of the publishers and people who are promoting the new versions. They're the "new kids on the block." The King James Bible people have not changed.

What Does "Perfect" Really Mean?

> **#253 Issue:** Samuel Gipp referred to the King James Bible as a "perfect" Bible. (Script, p. 54)

Comment by Dr. Waite: I would want to have his definition of "perfect" before commenting on the statement. I don't believe there are any "translation errors" in the King James Bible, but I have found at least 3 errors in the Oxford edition of the KJB which are correct in the Hebrew, in the original KJB of 1611 and in the Cambridge edition. Printers as well as translators are imperfect and subject to the same depravity as the rest of the world. I would rather put the "perfect" stamp on the Traditional Masoretic Hebrew text and the Received Greek texts that underlie our King James Bible. He is contrasting the "Majority Text" and the Nestles texts, so why not refer to the Textus Receptus underlying the KJB in this context?

Mark 16:9-20--Two "Most Reliable" MSS?

> **#254 Issue:** Arthur Farstad disagreed (and rightly so) with the NIV footnote on Mark 16:9-20 which stated: "The two most reliable early manuscripts do not have" these twelve verses. (Script, p. 54)

Comment by Dr. Waite: The note refers to manuscripts B (Vatican) and ℵ (Sinai). These two manuscripts are **not** "the most reliable." They are among the worst that ever saw the light of day! This is what is wrong with this note in the New International Version. I was glad to see Dr. Farstad side with the TR/KJB!

> **#255 Issue:** John Ankerberg asked Dr. Strouse to sum up his argument, but does not give him much time do so. (Script, p. 54)

Comment by Dr. Waite: If you will notice the official Script of these programs, all these other men had about **five inches** of space in this transcript to sum up their arguments. Dr. Strouse had only about **one and a half inches** of space and that's it. This is not fair. It is grossly unfair of John Ankerberg to allow him to be cut off in his summary final statement. He first allowed Arthur Farstad to talk and then John Ankerberg himself asked Don Wilkins for his **four inches** of summary.

#256 Issue: Arthur Farstad interrupted Dr. Strouse's summary statement twice, no less. (Script, p. 55)

Comment by Dr. Waite: Why didn't Arthur Farstad remain silent and let Dr. Strouse give his summation statement. Nobody interrupted him. Why does he interrupt Dr. Strouse?

The Faults of the Sinai Manuscript--א

#257 Issue: Don Wilkins told of how he "studied" manuscript Aleph (Sinai) for "several hours." He extolled the virtues of it and denied it had been corrected by at least "ten different editors" as Samuel Gipp correctly stated. (Script, p. 55)

Comment by Dr. Waite: The NASV man, Don Wilkins, contradicted Dr. Farstad who had just recently mentioned that the Vatican and Sinai manuscripts contradict one another over "3000 times" in the Gospels alone. Codex Sinaiticus (א) is very garbled and undependable. It is one of the most perverted of the Greek manuscripts we have. Dean John William Burgon mentions this in his book, *The Revision Revised,* Burgon has studied א (Sinai) for longer than Don Wilkins claims to have studied it. Dean Burgon stated that the Sinai manuscript (א) was the work of:

> "'at least ten different revisers,' who, from the vith to the xiith century, have been endeavouring to lick into shape a text which its original author left 'very rough'" [Dean John William Burgon, *The Last Twelve Verses of Mark*, p. 76.]

#258 Issue: Don Wilkins said, referring to Aleph (Sinai) manuscript: "I only saw a few pages of it." (Script, p. 55)

Comment by Dr. Waite: How can he make a fair analysis of this if he has only seen a few pages of it? Why did he boast so much if this is true?

#259 Issue: Don Wilkins proudly boasted concerning Aleph (Sinai) manuscript: "I'm the only one in the group, I suspect, that's had a chance to actually see it." (Script, p. 55)

Comment by Dr. Waite: There's no pride in his family. He has it all! He was boasting about the fact that he had actually seen Codex Sinaiticus which Tischendorf bought from the monks at St. Catherine's Convent. The monks were getting ready to burn it, either to bake bread, or to keep warm. They knew it was worthless trash. They had relegated it to a wastebasket position. Here Don Wilkins thinks he is somebody great because he has seen "a few pages" of this manuscript.

NASV Greek Text Not the "Best Evidence"

#260 Issue: Don Wilkins says of his Greek text underlying his NASV: "The reason we've got the text the way we have it is because we're going back to the best evidence." (Script, p. 55)

Comment by Dr. Waite: It is not the best evidence! The Sinai manuscript (א) is one of the worst manuscripts possible! The same could be correctly said about B (the Vatican manuscript).

The Dangers of the New Versions

#261 Issue: Dan Wallace asked the KJB men on the panel: "Are you afraid of these new translations because you think they're done by some kind of a conspiratorial team?" (Script, p. 55)

Comment by Dr. Waite: I'm not afraid of any of these perversions (the New American Version perversion, the New International Version perversion, or the New King James perversion). All I'm trying to do is to say that the King James Bible is the most accurate of all the versions which are out there. It is the only Bible which is taken from the superior and only proper Hebrew and Greek texts. It has superiorly qualified translators. It uses the superior and only proper technique of translation. Because of all of the preceding four reasons, it has superior and proper theology.

I am opposed to these other versions because they have false and inferior Hebrew and Greek texts, inferior translators, inferior translation technique, and inferior as well as heretical theology. The New American Standard and the New International, for instance, have a Greek Text (basically Westcott and Hort's Greek Text with a few changes) that differs from the text which underlies our King James Bible in over 5,604 places by my actual count. These changes, according to the footnotes of Dr. Frederick Scrivener, involve no less than 9,970 Greek words by my actual count. This is 30 Greek words short of 10,000. This is not necessarily a "conspiratorial team," although it might be. The paraphrasers have simply started out with the wrong foundation. Dan Wallace is a professor at Dallas Theological Seminary and not directly related to any of the versions under discussion. Why is he there? He doesn't seem to be defending any of them. He seems only to be debasing and diminishing the King James Bible.

#262 Issue: Dan Wallace asked of the three KJB men again: "Are you afraid that you're going to lose some of the basic doctrines?" (Script, p.

55)

> **Comment by Dr. Waite:** We certainly are going to lose some "basic doctrines." Because of the Greek New Testament textual changes found in these new versions, many "basic doctrines" have been affected. The "doctrines" in the New Testament alone which have been affected add up to 356 doctrinal passages. These men who say there are no doctrines which have been changed are dead wrong. In our book, *Defending The King James Bible*, in chapter 5 we have 158 examples of doctrinal changes in the false Greek texts of B and ℵ that are reflected in the false versions.

#263 Issue: Dan Wallace said that "those who represent the King James are very much afraid of the modern versions."(Script, p. 55)

> **Comment by Dr. Waite:** I am very strongly opposed to the "modern versions." I am afraid of what these false modern versions are doing and will do to the doctrines of God's Word. I am afraid because of the false doctrines that they teach and the true doctrines they omit. I am afraid because of the false Hebrew and Greek manuscripts from which they translate. And I am afraid because of the false paraphrase, dynamic translation technique which they use.

The Accuracy of the King James Bible

#264 Issue: Dan Wallace asked of the King James Bible: "Is it more accurate?" He answers: "No." (Script, p. 55)

> **Comment by Dr. Waite:** The King James Bible is more accurate than any of these perversions represented on this telecast. It is more accurate than the New International Version. It is more accurate than the New American Standard Version. It is more accurate than the New King James Version. It accurately represents and translates the proper Hebrew into English and the proper Greek into English not as these others do. If it were not more accurate how did I find **over 2,000** examples of addition, subtraction, or change in the New King James Version (comparing it to the Hebrew and to the Greek texts)? If the King James Bible is not more accurate than the New American Standard Version, how could I find **over 4,000** examples of addition, subtraction, or change from the Hebrew and Greek texts translating into English? If the King James Bible is not more accurate than the New International Version, how did I find **over 6,653** examples of addition, subtraction or change from the Hebrew and Greek texts? This does not stand to reason. When Dan Wallace says that the King James Bible is not more accurate than all the others, he is dead wrong. Time and time again, the King James Bible has out-translated all of these other versions so far as accuracy is concerned.

Is "All Truth" in All the Versions?

#265 Issue: Dan Wallace said: "The truth is still going to be there,

whether we use a new translation or an old translation." (Script, p. 55)

Comment by Dr. Waite: Truth is **not** there whether you use a new translation or an old translation. Truth is gone when you take the truth out of the Hebrew or out of the Greek texts. It is gone when you use the false technique of dynamic equivalency whereby the paraphraser can add, subtract, or otherwise change God's Words. This is certainly the case with these other versions. You can't have truth when you have 5,604 places where the New Testament Greek text of the new versions is in error from the Textus Receptus. This includes 9,970 Greek words.

This is found in the New International Version and, to a greater or lesser extent, in the New American Standard Version, and in the New King James Version. When you use the technique of dynamic equivalency you do not preserve truth. In the dynamic equivalency method of paraphrasing, you can add words that are not in the Hebrew and Words that are not in the Greek. You can subtract Words that are in the Hebrew and are in the Greek. You can change those Hebrew and Greek Words in any way you wish. Dynamic equivalency techniques do **not** preserve truth. It does not give us what God said in His Words. It gives us what "Dr. so and so thinks God **meant** by what He said." I want to know what God said. That, and only that is genuine "translation." We have such genuine "translation" in the King James Bible.

Doctrine Is Affected in the New Versions

#266 Issue: Dan Wallace ended the script by wrongly denying once again that doctrine is not affected in any of the versions. (Script, p. 55)

Comment by Dr. Waite: The concluding statement of this script by Dan Wallace was: *"No doctrine is affected between these two kinds of translations."* I've said before and I'll say it again: **Doctrine is affected!** 356 doctrinal passages are listed by Dr. Jack Moorman by these various versions and perversions because they have a different Greek text. I've listed 158 passages where doctrine has been affected in chapter 5 of my book, *Defending the King James Bible.*

Let's just take up a few doctrines which are affected. Turn over to 1 Timothy 3:16 where the King James properly translates with the proper Greek Text,

"And without controversy great is the mystery of godliness: **God** *was manifest in the flesh, justified in the Spirit, seen of angels, preached unto the Gentiles, believed on in the world, received up into glory."*

What does ℵ say (there is no B in I Timothy 3:16)? It changes "**God**" to "**He**" or "**Who**." What do the New International Version, the New American Standard Version, and the New King James Version in the footnotes do? They take away *"***God** *was manifest in the flesh."* Is this not doctrine? Would not Dr. Dan Wallace of Dallas Theological Seminary agree with me that this was serious doctrine? To take away "**God**" from I Timothy 3:16 is doctrine being changed. This word for God in the Greek is "*theos*" not "*hos*," or "*ho*."

Take a look at Matthew 18:11. The King James Bible accurately says, *"For the Son of man is come to save that which was lost."* B and א (the Vatican and Sinai which the NIV says are the most reliable manuscripts) omit this entire verse. The New International Version omits this verse, the New American Standard Version puts it in brackets, and the footnotes of the New King James also suggest that this verse should be omitted. Is this not doctrine? Why did the Son of Man come into this world? Dan Wallace should certainly agree with us that doctrine **is** effected in these versions and Greek texts. *"The Son of Man is come to save that which was lost"* tells why Jesus came.

Look at Luke 9:56 where the King James Bible accurately translates, ***"For the Son of man is not come to destroy men's lives, but to save {them}. And they went to another village."*** The first part of that verse is eliminated by B and א (the Vatican and Sinai manuscripts). The New International Version takes away the first part of that verse. The New American Standard Version takes it away. The New King James Version in the footnotes takes it away as well. This is important doctrine, is it not! It talks about the mission of the Lord Jesus Christ.

In Ephesians 3:9 the King James Bible accurately translates,
*"And to make all men see what is the fellowship of the mystery, which from the beginning of the world hath been hid in God, who created all things **by Jesus Christ**."*
Those words, "**by Jesus Christ**" are eliminated in B and א (Vatican and Sinai) and so they are wiped away in the New American Standard, the New International Version, and the footnotes of the New King James Version. Is this not important doctrine that the Lord Jesus Christ created all things? Certainly it is.

In John 6:47 the King James Version accurately translates, *"Verily, verily, I say unto you, He that believeth **on me** hath everlasting life."* The Greek manuscripts B and א take away the words "**on me**." So does the NIV, the NASV, and the NKJV in the footnotes. They just render this verse *"he who believes has everlasting life."* Believes what or whom? This is doctrine. It is wrong doctrine in these other versions and correct doctrine in the King James Bible.

These are just a few of the major doctrines that are denied or altered in the new versions in question. Consult Chapter V of my book, *Defending the King James Bible* for the list of 158 doctrinal passages. It is **B.F.T. #1594-P**, 352 pages, hardback, @ **$12.00 +P&H**. Consult *The Early Manuscripts and the Authorized Version--A Closer Look.* (**B.F.T. #1825** for a GIFT of **$15+P&H**) for the 356 doctrinal passages listed by Dr. Jack Moorman.

VIII.
COMMENTS ON THE GLOSSARY
Script, Pages G-1 To G-5

The following comments are taken from some of the definitions given in the "GLOSSARY" which are found in the Script, pp. G-1 to G-5. The "G" in the page number means that the material is found in the "GLOSSARY." Though all of these terms were not used in the telecasts or on the video cassettes, some of the definitions need to be refuted because they convey misleading information.

#267 Issue: "<u>Alexandrian</u> (text)--A text type found in certain early manuscripts from Egypt. Named from the capital city, Alexandria. Early Church Fathers used a text such as this." (Script, p. G-1)

Comment by Dr. Waite: This is a false and misleading definition. The early Church Fathers used the Textus Receptus kind of text much more frequently than they did the Alexandrian text. According to Dr. Jack Moorman's research (*Early Church Fathers*) 70% of the early Church Fathers' quotes were from the text which underlies our King James Bible, the Textus Receptus. Only 30% were from the so-called, Alexandrian text of Westcott and Hort (B and ℵ).

#268 Issue: Under <u>Arian, Arianism, and Arius</u> (d. 336), they give some good points on his heresies, but do not mention that B and Aleph were influenced by these heresies. (Script, p. G-1)

Comment by Dr. Waite: We believe that the revised text which underlies these modern versions (NIV, NASV, RSV, and the rest) came from Arian heretics. They denied the Trinity and the Deity of Christ and doctored the manuscripts accordingly wherever they could. They didn't have all the manuscripts in their hands, so they couldn't doctor all of them.

#269 Issue: "<u>Aland, Kurt</u>--German textual scholar who has co-edited the Nestle-Aland text since 1940 . . . ." (Script, p. G-1)

Comment by Dr. Waite: What they didn't say is that Kurt Aland is a German apostate. He is a not a believer in the Deity of Christ, His Blood atonement, or His bodily resurrection. He is a German rationalist. He principally specializes in the false texts that tend to support the Westcott and Hort text of B and ℵ which underlie these modern versions.

#270 Issue: "Autograph--. . . No autograph is known to exist, but accurate copies do." (Script, p. G-1)

Comment by Dr. Waite: We believe that the "accurate copies" are the copies of the Textus Receptus which underlie our King James Bible.

#271 Issue: "Bengel, J. A. (16871752)--A Lutheran minister and scholar who produced one of the first critical editions of the Greek New Testament." (Script, p. G-1)

Comment by Dr. Waite: That's true and it was a critical edition that did not follow the Textus Receptus, but rather the text of B and ℵ.

#272 Issue: "Beza, Theodore (1519-1605)--. . . Beza's 1598 edition was one of the chief sources for the KJV of 1611." (Script, p. G-1)

Comment by Dr. Waite: This is correct, but in the actual telecast some of the men denied that Beza's text was what the KJV 1611 was primarily based on. They said it was either the text of Erasmus or the *Complutensian Polyglot*. Neither of these two is correct.

#273 Issue: "Bombastus . . . Catholic humanist medical doctor . . . who was an acquaintance of Desiderius Erasmus. Bombastus held Gnostic views and was suspected of Arianism." (Script, p. G-1)

Comment by Dr. Waite: It appears that this statement is an attempt to smear Erasmus. They said: Bombastus "*was an acquaintance*" of Erasmus. Bombastus held Gnostic views and was suspected of Arianism. The implication might be that Erasmus also held Gnostic or Arian views which is entirely false.

#274 Issue: "Byzantine (text)--A text type found in those manuscripts which come from Greece and Western Turkey, the ancient empire of Byzantium." (Script, p. G-1)

Comment by Dr. Waite: First of all, I disagree that this is a "text type." There are no such things, only Greek manuscripts. The so-called Byzantine type of text (which is similar to the Textus Receptus) was not limited to Turkey and Greece. It came from every part of the then-known world. That is why over 99% of the manuscript evidence is in accord with the Textus Receptus manuscripts.

#275 Issue: "Burgon, John (1813-1888)--. . . was strongly opposed to the work of Westcott and Hort, serving with them on the committee for the Revised Version of 1881." (Script, p. G-1)

Comment by Dr. Waite: While it is true that Dean Burgon was *"strongly opposed to the work of Westcott and Hort,"* it is absolutely false to say that he was on the 1881 Revised Version committee! This misinformation is unfortunate.

#276 Issue: "Caesarean--A text type (see 'family') . . ."(Script, p. G-1)

Comment by Dr. Waite: I don't believe in such things as text types or "families." This is a figment of the imaginations of Westcott and Hort and their modern followers.

#277 Issue: "Comma Johanneum-- . . . 1 John 5:7b-8a . . ." They said of a manuscript containing this portion, "One was drawn up (!) and presented to Erasmus who reluctantly accepted the reading." (Script, pp. G-1, 2)

Comment by Dr. Waite: This is a false statement and leaves a false impression! It is in hundreds and hundreds of Latin manuscripts. For a full defense of its authenticity see Dr. Jack Moorman's 15-page summary (**B.F.T. #2249, 15 pages @ $1.50+P&H**) and/or Michael Maynard's large book (**B.F.T. #2008, 382 pages @ $32+P&H**) on this 1 John 5:7-8.

#278 Issue: "Complutensian Polyglot--An edition of the Greek Bible commissioned in 1502 by Catholic Cardinal Ximenes of Toledo, Spain. . . ." (Script, p. G-2)

Comment by Dr. Waite: They don't mention this, but the Complutensian Polyglot is in agreement with the Textus Receptus and stands with the text which underlies our King James Bible.

#279 Issue: "Conjectural emendation--A proposed change in the text of Scripture. When manuscripts do not agree or when a reading appears unlikely, in rare cases textual scholars make a conjecture as to the most likely reading of the original." (Script, p. G-2)

Comment by Dr. Waite: Conjecture or guess is completely out of place in any treating of the New Testament. Conjectural emendations are made repeatedly in the Old Testament *Biblia Hebraica* of Kittel and Stuttgart. It is also used repeatedly in the documentation of Westcott and Hort and modern critical text men of today.

#280 Issue: "Dynamic Equivalence--A technique of translation which attempts to reproduce the meaning of the original language rather than its form and structure." (Script, p. G-2)

Comment by Dr. Waite: This is not a technique of translation, by the way. It is paraphrase. If you don't reproduce the original language form and structure (including the words), you don't have translation, you have paraphrase. The dynamic equivalency adds to God's Words, subtracts from God's Words and changes God's Words in other ways.

#281 Issue: "Formal equivalence--A translation technique which aims primarily at reproducing the form and structure of the language, believing that the meaning is thereby most accurately communicated." (Script, p. G-2)

Comment by Dr. Waite: This is what the King James Bible has given us--the **forms** of the words as well as "verbal equivalence" giving us the words from Hebrew and Greek into English.

#282 Issue: "Family (textual family/text type)). **Refers to the kind of text which a manuscript is judged to be, based upon its geographical origin and its features. There are four families: Alexandrian (from Egypt), Western (from the western part of the Roman Empire), Byzantine (from Greece and Western Turkey), and Caesarean (from Jerusalem)." (Script, p. G-2)**

Comment by Dr. Waite: We believe that textual "families" are not really in existence. There are all different Greek texts and not "families." Dean John William Burgon said these families were like going into a cemetery with unmarked graves. You can't tell who is related to whom. You cannot yoke up one with another by way of family relationship.

#283 Issue: "Gnosticism--A theology which developed in the second century and threatened the Christian Church with doctrines which, among other things, denied the deity of Christ, the bodily resurrection, and salvation by grace alone." (Script, p. G-2)

Comment by Dr. Waite: Gnosticism permeates the Westcott and Hort type of Greek text. It permeates the B and ℵ manuscripts. It permeates the text on which the new versions and perversions are based. That's because Gnostics polluted and corrupted their Greek New Testament. Some of these false doctrines can be seen in the new versions because of such heretical corruptions.

#284 Issue: "Greek New Testament--The name given to the Greek text printed by the United Bible Societies since 1968. It is also known as the UBS text."(Script, p. G-2)

Comment by Dr. Waite: This is a Westcott and Hort type of text all the way. It follows closely B (Vatican) and ℵ (Sinai) textual readings and has now adopted the identical Greek text of Nestle-Aland Greek New Testament.

#285 Issue: "Higher criticism--The science of examining the background and source of the Bible. This field of study is misused by liberal critics to question and undermine the integrity and authenticity of Scripture through conjecture, supposition, hypothesis, and speculation." (Script, p. G-2)

Comment by Dr. Waite: The false methods of higher criticism have also infiltrated much of the lower (or textual) criticism. Westcott and Hort were heavily into higher criticism methodology as are some of the panelists.

#286 Issue: "Hort, F. J. A. (1828-1892)--New Testament scholar and textual critic who worked with B. F. Westcott in producing the Revised Version of 1881 and the seminal work in the field of textual criticism." (Script, p. G-2)

Comment by Dr. Waite: They failed to mention that he was an unbeliever, and a theological heretic and apostate. This is written as though Westcott and Hort were the only ones who produced the English Revised Version of 1881. This is not true at all. There were many other editors on that E.R.V. They also failed to mention that these two produced an error-ridden and false Greek text that was used, for the most part, in that E.R.V. of 1881. He is to be faulted because he used basically only B (the Vatican manuscript) and ℵ (the Sinai manuscript) instead of using all the evidence in his possession.

#287 Issue: "Inerrancy--The doctrine that asserts that the 66 books are, being God-breathed, without error of any kind in all that they affirm." (Script, p. G-2)

Comment by Dr. Waite: Not only "*all that they affirm,*" but also in "*all matters of which they speak.*" The Lausanne Covenant contained the phrase "*in all that they affirm*" and did NOT mean "*in all matters of which they speak.*" John Stott, the joint Chairman of that congress, said the Scriptures do not "affirm" all that they contain, hence cannot all be inerrant. I have written a complete analysis of this International Congress on World Evangelization (I.C.O.W.E.) where I discuss these matters. It is **B.F.T. #203, 254 pages, @ $25.00 + P&H.**

#288 Issue: "Paraphrase--A technique of translation which allows for extreme freedom in restating the original words of Scripture. An example is Kenneth Taylor's *The Living Bible.* It is not to be thought of as a translation." (Script, p. G-4)

Comment by Dr. Waite: Paraphrase is not "translation" any more than dynamic equivalence is "translation." Neither is the NIV or any other version which uses dynamic equivalency to be thought of as a translation. They are, to a greater or lesser degree, paraphrases.

#289 Issue: "Preservation--The doctrine that God will insure that His Word is guarded and kept safe from utter destruction. (see Matthew 5:18) (Script, p. G-4)

Comment by Dr. Waite: By limiting preservation only to keeping

God's Words safe "*from utter destruction*," these men on the panel who opposed the King James Bible did not believe that God even promised to preserve His **Words** in the original Hebrew or Greek. Therefore, they deny that the copies of those original language texts have been preserved.. I believe God's Hebrew and Greek Words were preserved in the Hebrew and Greek texts that underlie the King James Bible.

#290 Issue: "Revised Version (RV)--An English translation produced by Anglican scholars and first published in 1881. It was originally intended to be an updating of the KJV, but two scholars, B.F. Westcott and F. J. A. Hort, influenced the committee to adopt their Greek text and to produce a wholly new translation (which never met with public acceptance)." (Script, p. G-4)

Comment by Dr. Waite: That is true. Westcott and Hort forced their erroneous Greek text upon that E.R.V. of 1881 committee. It is the basis for the New Testament, for the most part, in our modern versions as well.

#291 Issue: "Reuchlin, Johannes (1455-1522)--German humanist scholar who was an expert in Latin, Greek and Hebrew (he was especially known as the great Hebraist of his day). . . ." (Script, p. G-4)

Comment by Dr. Waite: Reuchlin was important. He was the greatest Hebrew scholar of his day just as Erasmus was the greatest Greek scholar of his day.

#292 Issue: "Recension--A term used to describe the editorial work and textual product of a scribe that attempts to standardize a text by choosing certain readings among existing manuscripts and making changes in the text which seem called for in order to restore the original wording. The Byzantine Text is thought to be an early 4th century A.D. recension produced by Lucian of Antioch." (Script, p. G-4)

Comment by Dr. Waite: That is absolutely false! This has no historical background of any kind. Actually, the text of Westcott and Hort is a **recension**. The Byzantine Text is the original Greek words that go right back to Peter, Paul, John and the other authors. There is no historical proof whatsoever that a recension of the Greek text was made in either 250 A.D. or again in 350 A.D. which allegedly consolidated the Textus Receptus.

#293 Issue: "Scrivener, F. H. A. (1813-1891)--A British scholar and textual expert who wrote *Plain Introduction to the Criticism of the New Testament* (1851, 1874, 1883, 1894), a two-volume tome on textual criticism. Scrivener was a staunch defender of the Textus Receptus. (which see)." (Script, p. G-4)

Comment by Dr. Waite: We have reproduced the fourth edition of this book edited by Edward Miller. It is **B.F.T. #1285**, 920 large pages, @ $45 +P&H). You may get it from the Bible for Today if you are interested in having it. Scrivener was also on the English Revised Version Committee of 1881 and disputed with Westcott and Hort in most of their suggested changes to the Textus Receptus.

> **#294 Issue:** "Septuagint (now called the LXX)--A Greek translation of the Old Testament done over a period of time from 250 B.C. to perhaps 125 B.C., for the purpose of providing the Old Testament for the Jews who spoke Greek and no longer understood Hebrew." (Script, p. G-4)

Comment by Dr. Waite: I don't believe these dates are accurate. I think it is probably A.D. as a whole. I believe it was the firth column of Origen's Hexapla. Parts of it were no doubt made B.C., but not the entire Old Testament.

> **#295 Issue:** "Simon, Richard (1638-1712)--A French Catholic scholar who produced not only several volumes on textual criticism (which scholars today still use), but a critical edition of the Greek New Testament." (Script, p. G-4)

Comment by Dr. Waite: This critical edition follows the B and ℵ text much like a Westcott and Hort type of text.

> **#296 Issue:** "Sinaiticus--Also known as *Codex Aleph*. It is a 4th century manuscript discovered by Konstantin Tischendorf at St. Catherine's monastery at Mt. Sinai. It is considered by scholars to be the most important manuscript in existence." (Script, p. G-4)

Comment by Dr. Waite: Certainly the scholars are wrong. It is not *"the most important manuscript in existence."* It has 10 different correctors who tried to *"lick into shape"* (as Dean Burgon wrote) that which was very rough. It was ready to be scrapped by the monks. They were ready to burn it. Tischendorf was ready to buy it. We believe that it vies with Manuscript B (Vatican) for being one of the most obnoxious and false manuscripts known to the manuscript history today.

> **#297 Issue:** "Stephens, Robert (or Robert Etienne) (1503-1559)--A royal printer in France who published four editions of the Textus Receptus, the third and fourth (because it was identical to the third) editions followed Erasmus' fourth and fifth editions. His text is known as the Stephens text. Stephens was also the first to include modern verse divisions (having created them) in the Greek N.T." (Script, p. G-4)

Comment by Dr. Waite: His most popular edition was the 1550 edition which was the basis of the *Englishman's Interlinear Greek/English New Testament*. This is **B.F.T. #186**, 811 pages, @ $26.00 +P&H by Dr. Berry.

#298 Issue: "<u>Textual criticism</u>--the science of examining and evaluating the pertinent sources for the Greek NT in order to reconstruct the original text." (Script, pp. G-4)

Comment by Dr. Waite: I believe we have the original text in copy form of the Textus Receptus that underlies the King James Bible. Therefore I believe we should cease from "textual criticism." We don't need it. It has only taken us farther away from the true original Greek text rather than getting us closer to it.

#299 Issue: "<u>Textus Receptus</u> (also called the TR)--The name given to the kind of text printed in the 16th and early 17th centuries, first published by Desiderius Erasmus in 1516. The term derives from a statement found in the 1637 Elziver edition of this text. There are over 30 editions of the Textus Receptus and no two are completely identical." (Script, pp. G-4, 5)

Comment by Dr. Waite: It is misleading to say that the Textus Receptus was "**first published**" by Desiderius Erasmus. If they mean the first printed edition, all right. However, the Textus Receptus was started by Paul and Peter and John and the other original authors of the New Testament. These manuscripts (over 5,210) were not started or founded by Erasmus, he simply collated some of these manuscripts. The Textus Receptus was not started by any man. It is found in the over 5,210 Greek manuscripts that we now have preserved for us. Each of these manuscripts of the Traditional Text or Received Greek Text are virtually identical. Certainly there are minor variations in spelling of names, etc., but the miracle of it all is that they are practically the same. This cannot be said of B and ℵ that contradict each other over 3,000 times in the Gospels alone, as Herman Hoskier has so painstakingly found in his *Codex B and its Allies*. This has been re-printed in the Bible for Today format. It is **B.F.T. #1643**, 924 pages @ **$46+P&H.**

#300 Issue: "<u>Variant</u>--A reading found in one manuscript that differs from a reading found in another manuscript. It is the task of textual experts to decide between variants which is the original." (Script, p. G-5)

Comment by Dr. Waite: Notice that their definition states that "*textual experts*" are the only people who can tell you which "variant" is the correct one. I believe that the Textus Receptus that underlies the King James Bible is the original copy of what God has written down. I also believe that every born again, saved Christian has the right and privilege of entering into this process. We should <u>never</u> leave the determination of our Bible to the "**textual experts**."

#301 Issue: "<u>Vaticanus</u>--Also known as Codex B. It is a fourth century manuscript housed in the Vatican library since 1475. Although not as widely accepted as *Codex Aleph (Sinaiticus)*, it is considered a valuable early

manuscript." (Script, p. 5)

Comment by Dr. Waite: That is false! The Vatican manuscript is considered to be of much greater value than ℵ (Sinai.) Westcott and Hort both said that B is the very best manuscript in existence. They try to get ℵ (Sinai) to agree with B (Vatican) if possible, but if not, they prefer B all alone. This is extremely misleading in this glossary.

#302 Issue: "Westcott, B. F. (1825-1901)--Anglican scholar and textual expert, was with F. J. A. Hort the leader in textual criticism in the 19th century." (Script, p. G-5)

Comment by Dr. Waite: He was considered a textual expert by his followers, but not by me. He used conjecture and false methods of textual criticism that were spurious. He didn't believe in the Textus Receptus, and did everything in his lying power to dethrone it. The definition does not say that he was a heretic, and a theological apostate which he was.

#303 Issue: The Fairness or Lack of Fairness of this Series. Was their fairness and balance in these videos and telecasts?

Comment by Dr. Waite: What was the fairness or report of this John Ankerberg telecast? I have a two page letter which I sent to John Ankerberg telling him why I changed my mind about coming on this telecast. If you would like to receive this you may.

Here is the participation data for all 9 speakers: There was a total of 160 minutes in these eight programs. There were a total of 656 total inches of space on the Script. <u>John Ankerberg</u> had 168 inches of space (he was the host against the King James Bible), 26% of the time, he spoke on the average of 42 minutes. <u>James White</u> (a writer and anti-King James Bible man) had 112 inches of space, 17% of the time, 27 minutes. <u>Dan Wallace</u> (anti-King James Bible man from Dallas Seminary) had 88 inches of space, spoke 14% of the time, 22 minutes. <u>Kenneth Barker</u> (against the King James Bible, representing the New International Version) 76 inches of space, 12% of the time, 19 minutes. <u>Samuel Gipp</u> (pro-King James man) had 67 inches of space, 10% of the time, 16 minutes. <u>Dr. Joseph Chambers</u> (pro-King James man) 64 inches of space, 8% of the time, 13 minutes. <u>Arthur Farstad</u> (anti-King James Bible and for the New King James Version) 42 inches of space, 6% of the time, 10 minutes. <u>Don Wilkins</u> (against the King James Bible and for the New American Standard Version) 28 inches of space, 4%, 6 minutes. <u>Dr. Thomas Strouse</u> (for the King James Bible) 21 inches of space, 3%, only 5 minutes out of 160 total minutes.

Look at the fairness for the speakers on both sides. If you add up all the six speakers against the King James Bible, they had 514 inches of space, 79% of the time, 126 minutes. What about the pro-King James people? They had only 142 inches of space, 21 % of the time, and 34 minutes. <u>**126 minutes were given to the**</u>

anti-King James people and only 34 minutes were give to the pro-King James people. This was not fair and I believe that this is important to point out. I asked John Ankerberg if it was going to be fair and he assured me that it would be.

I have also answered the Script on my weekly radio broadcasts. These radio cassettes are available from the Bible For Today. There are 9 cassettes, 2 hours each, 18 hours 36 broadcasts available as **BFT/110-118 @ $30**. If you are interested in such an audio discussion or would like **extra copies of this book**, write us or phone us for details at 1-800-JOHN 10:9.

"Therefore, my beloved brethren, be ye stedfast, unmoveable, always abounding in the work of the Lord, forasmuch as ye know that your labour is not in vain in the Lord."
(1 Corinthians 15:58)

INDEX OF CERTAIN WORDS AND PHRASES

[NOTE: The phrases used in this INDEX might be used by other speakers, and are not necessarily the opinions of the author of this study. The words in BOLD FACE TYPE are the run-in headings found throughout the book. They indicate the major themes of the book. DAW]

INDEX OF SCRIPTURE REFERENCES

About the Author

The author of this booklet, Dr. D. A. Waite, received a B.A. (Bachelor of Arts) in classical Greek and Latin from the University of Michigan in 1948, a Th.M. (Master of Theology), with high honors, in New Testament Greek Literature and Exegesis from Dallas Theological Seminary in 1952, an M.A. (Master of Arts) in Speech from Southern Methodist University in 1953, a Th.D. (Doctor of Theology), with honors, in Bible Exposition from Dallas Theological Seminary in 1955, and a Ph.D. in Speech from Purdue University in 1961. He holds both New Jersey and Pennsylvania teacher certificates in Greek and Language Arts.

He has been a teacher in the areas of Greek, Hebrew, Bible, Speech, and English for over thirty-five years in nine schools, including one junior high, one senior high, three Bible institutes, two colleges, two universities, and one seminary. He served his country as a Navy Chaplain for five years on active duty; pastored two churches; was Chairman and Director of the Radio and Audio-Film Commission of the American Council of Christian Churches; since 1971, has been Founder, President, and Director of THE BIBLE FOR TODAY; since 1978, has been President of the DEAN BURGON SOCIETY; has produced over 700 other studies, booklets, cassettes, or VCR's on various topics; and is heard on both a five-minute daily and thirty-minute weekly radio program IN DEFENSE OF TRADITIONAL BIBLE TEXTS, presently on 25 stations. Dr. and Mrs. Waite have been married since 1948; they have four sons, one daughter, and, at present, eight grandchildren.

Order Blank (p.1)

Name:_____

Address:_____

City & State:_____Zip:_____

*Credit Card #:*_____*Expires:*_____

[ ] Send *Foes of the King James Bible Refuted* by DAW ($9
    +$4 S&H) A perfect bound book, 164 pages in length.

[ ] Send *The Revision Revised* by Dean Burgon ($25 + $4)
    A hardback book, 640 pages in length.

[ ] Send *The Last 12 Verses of Mark* by Dean Burgon ($15+$4)
    A perfect bound paperback book 400 pages in length.

[ ] Send *The Traditional Text* by Dean Burgon ($16 + $4)
    A hardback book, 384 pages in length.

[ ] Send *Summary of Traditional Text* by Dr. Waite ($3 + $2)

[ ] Send *Summary of Causes of Corruption*, DAW ($3+$2)

[ ] Send *The Causes of Corruption* by Dean Burgon ($15 + $4)
    A hardback book, 360 pages in length.

[ ] Send *Inspiration and Interpretation*, Dean Burgon ($25+$4)

[ ]Send *Contemporary Eng. Version Exposed*, DAW ($3+$2)

[ ] Send the "DBS Articles of Faith & Organization" (N.C.)

[ ] Send Brochure #1: "1,000 Titles Defending KJB/TR"
    (N.C.)

Send or Call Orders to:
THE BIBLE FOR TODAY
900 Park Ave., Collingswood, NJ 08108
Phone: 609-854-4452; FAX:--2464; Orders: 1-800 JOHN 10:9
E-Mail Orders: BFT@BibleForToday.org; Credit Cards OK

Order Blank (p.2)

Name:_____

Address:_____

City & State:_____Zip:_____

Credit Card#:_____Expires:_____

Other Materials on the KJB & T.R.

[ ] Send *Westcott & Hort's Greek Text & Theory Refuted by Burgon's Revision Revised—Summarized* by Dr. D. A. Waite ($3.00 + $3 S&H)

[ ] Send *Defending the King James Bible* by Dr.Waite $12+$4 A hardback book, indexed with study questions.

[ ] Send *Guide to Textual Criticism* by Edward Miller ($7 + $4)

[ ] Send *Heresies of Westcott & Hort* by Dr. Waite ($4+$3)

[ ] Send *Westcott's Denial of Resurrection*, Dr. Waite ($4+$3)

[ ] Send *Four Reasons for Defending KJB* by DAW ($2+$3)

[ ] Send *Vindicating Mark 16:9-20* by Dr. Waite ($3 + $3)

[ ] Send *Dean Burgon's Confidence in KJB* by DAW ($3+$3)

[ ] Send *Readability of A.V. (KJB)* by D. A. Waite, Jr. ($5 + $3)

[ ] Send *NIV Inclusive Language Exposed* by DAW ($4+$3)

[ ] Send *23 Hours of KJB Seminar (4 videos) by DAW ($50.00)*

Send or Call Orders to:
THE BIBLE FOR TODAY
900 Park Ave., Collingswood, NJ 08108
Phone: 609-854-4452; FAX:--2464; Orders: 1-800 JOHN 10:9
E-Mail Orders: BFT@BibleForToday.org; Credit Cards OK

Order Blank (p.3)

Name:_____

Address:_____

City & State:_____Zip:_____

Credit Card #:_____Expires:_____

More Materials on the KJB &T.R.

[ ] **Send** *Scrtvener's Greek New Testament Underlying the King James Bible*, **hardback, $14+$4 S&H**

[ ] **Send** *Why Not the King James Bible?--An Answer to James White's KJVO Book* **by Dr. K. D. DiVietro, $9+$4 S&H**

[ ] **Send** *Forever Settled--Bible Documents & History Survey* **by Dr. Jack Moorman, $21+$4 S&H**

[ ] **Send** *Early Church Fathers & the A.V.--A Demonstration* **by Dr. Jack Moorman, $6 + $4 S&H.**

[ ] **Send** *When the KJB Departs from the So-Called "Majority Text"* **by Dr. Jack Moorman, $16 + $4 S&H**

[ ] **Send** *Missing in Modern Bibles--Nestle-Aland & NIV Errors* **by Dr. Jack Moorman, $8 + $4 S&H**

[ ] **Send** *The Doctrinal Heart of the Bible--Removed from Modern Versions* **by Dr. Jack Moorman, VCR, $15 +$4 S&H**

[ ] **Send** *Modern Bibles--The Dark Secret* **by Dr. Jack Moorman, $3 + $2 S&H**

[ ] **Send** *Early Manuscripts and the A.V.--A Closer Look,* **by Dr. Jack Moorman, $15 + $4 P&H**

Send or Call Orders to:
THE BIBLE FOR TODAY
900 Park Ave., Collingswood, NJ 08108
Phone: 609-854-4452; FAX:--2464; Orders: 1-800 JOHN 10:9
E-Mail Orders: BFT@BibleForToday.org; Credit Cards OK

My Bible

When I am tired, the Bible meets my need.
When I'm perplexed, Its wisdom great I heed.
When I am tossed, Its promises I read.
When I am faint, on Manna sweet I feed.

When I am sad, my Bible is my stay.
When I'm afraid, It comforts me alway.
When I'm alone, my Bible's near at hand.
When I must fight, His Word doth give command.

When I would serve, my Bible tells me where.
When I would sing, It gives me both song and air.
When I would give, the Bible tells my share.
When I would love, my Bible helps me care.

When I would run, the Bible sets the pace.
When I must pause, it shows a quiet place.
And when I yearn to see my Saviour's face,
His lovely form is outlined there in Grace.

When I am old, the Bible is my friend.
When I am weak, upon It I depend.
When I must die, It blesses to the end.
All through my life, I will Its Truth defend.

By Gertrude Grace Sanborn
[The author's mother-in-law]

the
BIBLE
FOR
TODAY

900 Park Avenue
Collingswood, NJ 08108
Phone: 609-854-4452

B.F.T. #2777

ISBN #1-56848-010-5